The Giver

by Lois Lowry

Literature Guide
Written by Angela Frith Antrim
for *Secondary Solutions*®

ISBN-10: 0-9816243-1-6
ISBN-13: 978-0-9816243-1-0

The *First* Solution for the Secondary Teacher®
www.4secondarysolutions.com

The Giver Literature Guide
Table of Contents

About This Literature Guide

Secondary Solutions is the endeavor of a high school English teacher who could not seem to find appropriate materials to help her students master the necessary concepts at the secondary level. She grew tired of spending countless hours researching, creating, writing, and revising lesson plans, worksheets, quizzes, tests and extension activities to motivate and inspire her students, and at the same time, address those ominous content standards! Materials that were available were either juvenile in nature, skimpy in content, or were moderately engaging activities that did not come close to meeting the content standards on which her students were being tested. Frustrated and tired of trying to get by with inappropriate, inane lessons, she finally decided that if the right materials were going to be available to her and other teachers, she was going to have to make them herself! Mrs. Bowers set to work to create one of the most comprehensive and innovative Literature Guide sets on the market. Joined by a middle school teacher with 21 years of secondary school experience, **Secondary Solutions** began, and has matured into a specialized team of intermediate and secondary teachers who have developed for you a set of materials unsurpassed by all others.

Before the innovation of **Secondary Solutions**, materials that could be purchased offered a reproducible student workbook and a separate set of teacher materials at an additional cost. Other units provided the teacher with student materials only, and very often, the content standards were ignored. **Secondary Solutions** provides all of the necessary materials for complete coverage of the literature units of study, including author biographies, pre-reading activities, numerous and varied vocabulary and comprehension activities, study-guide questions, graphic organizers, literary analysis and critical thinking activities, essay-writing ideas, extension activities, quizzes, unit tests, alternative assessment, and much, much more. Each Guide is designed to address the unique learning styles and comprehension levels of every student in your classroom. All materials are written and presented at the grade level of the learner, and include ***extensive coverage of the content standards.*** As an added bonus, all teacher materials are *included!*

As a busy teacher, you don't have time to waste reinventing the wheel. You want to get down to the business of *teaching*! With our professionally developed teacher-written Literature Guides, **Secondary Solutions** has provided you with the answer to your time management problems, while saving you hours of tedious and exhausting work. Our Guides will allow you to focus on the most important aspects of teaching—the personal, one-on-one, hands-on instruction you enjoy most—the reason you became a teacher in the first place.

The *First* Solution for the Secondary Teacher®
www.4secondarysolutions.com

How to Use Our Literature Guides

Our Literature Guides are based upon the *National Council of the Teachers of English* and the *International Readers Association's* national English/Language Arts Curriculum and Content Area Standards. The materials we offer allow you to teach the love and full enjoyment of literature, while still addressing the concepts upon which your students are assessed.

These Guides are designed to be used in their sequential entirety, or may be divided into separate parts. Not all activities must be used, but to achieve full comprehension and mastery of the skills involved, it is recommended that you utilize everything each Guide has to offer. Most importantly, you now have a variety of valuable materials to choose from, and you are not forced into extra work.

There are several distinct categories within each Literature Guide:

- ***Exploring Expository Writing***—Worksheets designed to address the exploration and analysis of functional and/or informational materials. For example:
  - ✓ *Author Biography*
  - ✓ *Biographies of non-fiction characters*
  - ✓ *Relevant news and magazine articles, etc.*
  - ✓ *Articles on historical context*
- ***Comprehension Check***—Similar to *Exploring Expository Writing*, but designed for comprehension of narrative text—study questions designed to guide students *as they read the text.*
- ***Standards Focus***—Worksheets and activities that directly address the content standards and allow students extensive practice in literary skills and analysis. *Standards Focus* activities are found within every chapter or section. Some examples:
  - ✓ *Figurative Language*
  - ✓ *Irony*
  - ✓ *Flashback*
- ***Assessment Preparation***—Vocabulary activities which emulate the types of vocabulary/ grammar proficiency on which students are tested in state and national assessments. *Assessment Preparation* activities are found within every chapter or section. Some examples:
  - ✓ *Context Clues*
  - ✓ *Connotation/Denotation*
  - ✓ *Word Roots*
- ***Quizzes and Tests***—Quizzes are included for each chapter or designated section; final tests as well as alternative assessment are available at the end of each Guide. These include:
  - ✓ *Multiple Choice*
  - ✓ *Matching*
  - ✓ *Short Response*
- ***Pre-Reading, Post-Reading Activities, Essay/Writing Ideas plus Sample Rubrics***—Each Guide also has its own unique pre-reading, post-reading, essay/writing ideas, and alternative assessment activities.

Each Guide contains handouts and activities with varied levels of difficulty. We know that not all students are alike—nor are all teachers. We hope you can effectively utilize every aspect our Literature Guides have to offer—we want to make things easier on you! If you need additional assistance, please email us at info@4secondarysolutions.com. Thank you for choosing Secondary Solutions®.

Sample Teacher's Agenda and Notes

Week One
Day One: Begin introducing themes and elements of the novel through *Pre-Reading Ideas and Activities* (pg. 116). Introduce the *Author Biography* activity (pgs. 9-10) and complete the *Standards Focus: Genre* activity (pgs. 11-12). You may want to assign an additional *Pre-Reading Activity* to students who could benefit from delving deeper into the novel's themes.
Day Two: Continue introducing themes of the novel through *Pre-Reading Ideas and Activities* (pg. 116). Introduce the *Anticipation/Reaction Guide* (pgs. 17-19), and take time to discuss some of the themes presented in it. Allocate time for students to work on other *Pre-Reading Activities.*
Day Three: Read and discuss the *Allusions and Terminology* (pgs. 13-15), as well as the *Vocabulary List* (pg. 17) for reference. You can either have students find their own definitions in a dictionary, or read the definitions to them, using pages 114-115 for reference. You may also want to allocate time for students to work on other *Pre-Reading Activities.*
Day Four: Introduce/explain *Note-Taking and Summarizing Activity* on pages 20-21. Review vocabulary for Chapters 1-2 (pg. 17). Begin reading Chapter 1 and answering the *Comprehension Check* questions (pg. 23).
Day Five: Read Chapters 1-2, completing *Note-Taking and Summarizing* (pg. 22) and answering *Comprehension Check* questions (pg. 23).

Week Two
Day One: Discuss *Comprehension Check* questions for Chapters 1-2 and have students complete *Standards Focus: Foreshadowing* (pgs. 24-25).
Day Two: Complete *Assessment Preparation: Punctuation, Capitalization, Spelling, and Grammar* (pgs. 26-27); administer *Quiz: Chapters 1-2* (pg. 88).
Day Three: Review vocabulary for Chapters 3-4 (pg. 16). Begin reading Chapter 3, completing *Note-Taking* (pg. 28) and answering *Comprehension Check* questions (pg. 30).
Day Four: Finish reading Chapters 3-4, completing *Note-Taking* (pg. 29) and answering *Comprehension Check* questions (pg. 30).
Day Five: Discuss *Comprehension Check* questions for Chapters 3-4 and have students complete *Standards Focus: Point of View* (pgs. 31-32).

Week Three
Day One: Assign *Assessment Preparation: Word Origins—Etymology* (pgs. 33-34); give *Quiz- Chapters 3-4* (pg. 89).
Day Two: Give *Vocabulary Quiz: Chapters 1-4* (pg. 90); review vocabulary for Chapters 5-6 (pg. 16); begin reading Chapter 5, completing *Note-Taking* (pg. 35) and answering the *Comprehension Check* questions (pg. 37).
Day Three: Finish reading Chapters 5-6, completing *Note-Taking and Summarizing* (pg. 36) and answering the *Comprehension Check* questions (pg. 37).
Day Four: Discuss *Comprehension Check* questions Chapters 5-6 and have students complete *Standards Focus: Symbolism* (pgs. 38-39).
Day Five: Assign *Assessment Preparation: Parts of Speech* (pgs. 40-41) and give *Quiz: Chapters 5-6* (pg. 91).

Week Four
Day One: Review vocabulary for Chapters 7-8 (pg. 16); begin reading Chapter 7, completing *Note-Taking* (pg. 42) and answering the *Comprehension Check* questions (pg. 44).

Day Two: Finish reading Chapters 7-8, completing *Note-Taking and Summarizing* (pg. 43) and answering the *Comprehension Check* questions (pg. 44).
Day Three: Discuss *Comprehension Check* questions Chapters 7-8 and have students complete *Standards Focus: Setting and Problem* (pgs. 45-46).
Day Four: Assign *Assessment Preparation: Vocabulary in Context* (pgs. 47-48) and give *Quiz: Chapters 7-8* (pg. 92).
Day Five: Give *Vocabulary Quiz: Chapters 5-8* (pg. 93); review vocabulary for Chapters 9-10 (pg. 16); begin reading Chapter 9, completing *Note-Taking* (pg. 49) and answering *Comprehension Check* questions (pg. 51).

Week Five
Day One: Finish reading Chapters 9-10, completing *Note-Taking* (pg. 50) and answering the *Comprehension Check* questions (pg. 51).
Day Two: Discuss *Comprehension Check* questions Chapters 9-10 (pg. 51) and have students complete *Standards Focus: Imagery* (pgs. 52-53).
Day Three: Assign *Assessment Preparation: Verb Tense and Agreement* (pgs. 54-55) and give *Quiz: Chapters 9-10* (pg. 94).
Day Four: Review vocabulary for Chapters 11-12 (pg. 16); begin reading Chapter 11, completing *Note-Taking* (pg. 56) and answering *Comprehension Check* questions (pg. 58).
Day Five: Finish reading Chapters 11-12, completing *Note-Taking* (pg. 57) and answering the *Comprehension Check* questions (pg. 58).

Week Six
Day One: Discuss *Comprehension Check* questions Chapters 11-12 (pg. 58) and have students complete *Standards Focus: Elements of Style* (pgs. 59-60).
Day Two: Assign *Assessment Preparation: Synonyms and Antonyms* (pg. 61) and give *Quiz: Chapters 11-12* (pg. 95).
Day Three: Give *Vocabulary Quiz: Chapters 9-12* (pg. 96); review vocabulary for Chapters 13-14 (pg. 16); begin reading Chapter 13, completing *Note-Taking* (pg. 62) and answering *Comprehension Check* questions (pg. 64).
Day Four: Finish reading Chapters 13-14, completing *Note-Taking* (pg. 63) and answering the *Comprehension Check* questions (pg. 64).
Day Five: Discuss *Comprehension Check* questions Chapters 13-14 (pg. 64) and have students complete *Standards Focus: Conflict* (pgs. 65-66).

Week Seven
Day One: Assign *Assessment Preparation: Vocabulary Extension* (pg. 67) and give *Quiz: Chapters 13-14* (pg. 97).
Day Two: Review vocabulary for Chapters 15-17 (pg. 16); begin reading Chapters 15-16, completing *Note-Taking* (pg. 68) and answering *Comprehension Check* questions (pg. 70).
Day Three: Finish reading Chapters 15-17, completing *Note-Taking* (pg. 69) and answering the *Comprehension Check* questions (pg. 70).
Day Four: Discuss *Comprehension Check* questions Chapters 15-17 (pg. 70) and have students complete *Standards Focus: Theme* (pgs. 71-73). You may wish to do the first example as a class, have students pair or group to do #2, then have them complete the remainder of the activity individually.
Day Five: Assign *Assessment Preparation: Punctuation* (pgs. 74-75) and give *Quiz: Chapters 15-17* (pg. 98).

Week Eight

Day One: Give *Vocabulary Quiz: Chapters 13-17* (pg. 99); review vocabulary for Chapters 18-20 (pg. 16); begin reading Chapters 18-19, completing *Note-Taking* (pg. 76) and answering *Comprehension Check* questions (pg. 78).
Day Two: Finish reading Chapters 18-20, completing *Note-Taking* (pg. 77) and answering the *Comprehension Check* questions (pg. 78).
Day Three: Discuss *Comprehension Check* questions Chapters 18-20 (pg. 78) and have students complete *Standards Focus: Character Development* (pgs. 79-80).
Day Four: Assign *Assessment Preparation: Precise Word Choice* (pgs. 81-82) and give *Quiz: Chapters 18-20* (pg. 100).
Day Five: Review vocabulary for Chapters 21-23 (pg. 16); begin reading Chapter 21, completing *Note-Taking* (pg. 83) and answering the *Comprehension Check* questions (pg. 85).

Week Nine

Day One: Finish reading Chapters 21-23, completing *Note-Taking* (pg. 84) and answering the *Comprehension Check* questions (pg. 85).
Day Two: Discuss *Comprehension Check* questions Chapters 21-23 (pg. 85) and have students complete *Standards Focus: Elements of Plot* (pg. 86).
Day Three: Assign *Assessment Preparation: Sentence Structure* (pg. 87) and give *Quiz: Chapters 21-23* (pg. 101) and *Vocabulary Quiz: Chapters 18-23* (pg. 102).
Day Four: Review the novel by revisiting students' *Note-Taking Guides* and discussing the *Comprehension Check Questions.* Assign or let students select a *Post-Reading Activity* (pg. 117) or writing assignment from *Essay/ Writing Ideas* (pg. 118).
Day Five: Give either version of the *Final Test* (pgs. 103-106 or pgs. 107-110) or some form of *Alternative Assessment* (pg. 117). Have students write an essay from the *Essay/ Writing Ideas* (pg. 118). You may want to set aside an additional class period for students to share their completed Post-Reading Activities or Alternative Assessments.

As mentioned on page 5, not all activities and worksheets in this guide must be used. They are here to help you, so that you have some options to work with. Feel free to use all or only a few of the worksheets and activities from this guide. Here are a few notes about this guide:

1. Page numbers referred to in this Literature Guide are from the Dell Laurel-Leaf edition from Random House Children's Books, a division of Random House, Inc., © 1993.
2. Both the *Note-Taking and Summarizing* activities and *Comprehension Check* questions are there to help your students get the most out of the novel. Depending upon your students and their needs, you may want to have them only take notes, only answer questions, alternate, or do both.
3. *Post-Reading and Alternative Assessment* ideas are located on page 117. Again, these are suggestions only. These project ideas can be used in addition to a written test or in place of it. A *Project Rubric* is located on page 119.
4. Essay ideas are located on page 118. Often, in addition to their written test, having students choose ONE topic from 2-3 essay topics chosen by the teacher in advance works well. Many of these options can also work well for a process essay or writing project. Some teachers allow students to earn extra credit using Post-Reading Activities or Essay/ Writing Ideas. A *Response to Literature Rubric* is on pages 120-121.

Name ____________________ Period __________

Standards Focus: Author Biography
Lois Lowry

Lois Lowry was born in Hawaii on March 20, 1937. She was born the middle child in a family of three children, a blessing which Lowry believes allowed her the freedom to read and revel in her imagination.

Lowry's father was a career American military officer, and the family moved frequently throughout the author's childhood. Lowry also lived in New York and Pennsylvania in her youth.

In 1948, at eleven years old, Lowry's family moved to an Americanized military community in Tokyo, Japan. Even though the family lived in the midst of a thriving Asian city, they resided in an American-style house with American neighbors, saw American movies, and attended an American school. Even though the author lived in an insular American community, she was very curious about her Japanese neighbors. In *The Giver*, Lowry draws upon her memories of clandestinely exploring the Japanese neighborhoods of Tokyo on her bicycle. This experience partially forms the basis of Elsewhere in the novel.

Lowry returned to New York City for high school and attended Brown University in Rhode Island for college. In 1956, at age nineteen, Lowry left Brown to marry naval officer Donald Lowry. The Lowry family moved frequently and had four children, two daughters and two sons.

The family settled in Maine, and Lowry completed her degree in English Literature at the University of Southern Maine in 1972. The author began working as a freelance journalist and published her first realistic fiction novel, *A Summer to Die*, in 1977, the same year that she and her husband divorced.

Lowry continued to write and began publishing the *Anastasia Krupnik* series in 1979. In 1989, Lowry won her first Newbery Medal for the historical fiction novel *Number the Stars* which tackles the Nazi occupation of Denmark during World War II. In 1993, the author won her second Newbery medal for her fantasy novel *The Giver* which discusses a futuristic, utopian society that goes terribly wrong. Even though Lowry's novels vary greatly in time period and **genre**, they all contain the same basic theme of the importance of nurturing human connections.

Lowry currently divides her time between Cambridge, Massachusetts and an old farmhouse in Maine. She enjoys reading, gardening, knitting, and spending time with her grandchildren.

genre: a type or category of artistic work, separated by similar subject, style, theme, etc.

Name ____ Period ___________

Standards Focus: Exploring Expository Writing—Author Biography

***Directions**: Using the biographical information about Lois Lowry, answer the following questions. Write the letter of the correct answer on the lines provided.*

1. ______What is the author's purpose in writing this biography of Lois Lowry?
   a. to tell the reader an entertaining story about Lois Lowry
   b. to persuade the reader to read one of Lois Lowry's books
   c. to provide information about Lois Lowry
   d. to describe Lois Lowry's childhood

2. ______Based on the information in the first two paragraphs, the reader can conclude that:
   a. Lois Lowry did not enjoy moving during her childhood.
   b. Lois Lowry had a close relationship with her family.
   c. Lois Lowry enjoyed living in New York.
   d. none of the above

3. ______Lowry's time living in Japan is important because:
   a. she learned to speak Japanese
   b. it influenced her writing of *The Giver*
   c. she enjoyed exploring Tokyo
   d. she made many friends in Japan

4. ______Where would be the BEST place in the biography to insert information about other books written by the author?
   a. in paragraph six
   b. add an additional paragraph between paragraphs six and seven
   c. in paragraph five
   d. in paragraph four

***Directions**: Answer the following questions using complete sentences.*

5. List the two books for which Lowry was awarded the Newbery Medal. Also, include the year in which she won each award. ____

____

6. The term *genre* is used in this biography. Explain in your own words what a literary genre is. Use the Internet or other source to find out about the different genres in which Lois Lowry wrote and list three of them here.______________________________

____

____

____

____

Name ____ Period ____________

Standards Focus: Genre
Fantasy, Science Fiction, and Dystopia

Lois Lowry's *The Giver* occurs in an other-worldly society which exists only in the author's imagination. The novel contains elements of traditional fantasy and science fiction to create the author's fictional community.

Fantasy novels take place in a world that does not and cannot exist on earth. They frequently incorporate magic or supernatural forces into the plot, theme, and setting. Fairy tales and myths often draw on magical themes, but modern fantasy literature really began with George MacDonald's *The Princess and the Goblin* and *Phantastes.* In the 20th century, authors created "lost" worlds, an aspect that Lowry incorporates in *The Giver*, in classic children's fantasies such as Baum's *Wizard of Oz* and Barrie's *Peter Pan.* Most fantasy novels were classified as children's literature until Lewis's *Chronicles of Narnia* and Tolkien's *The Lord of the Rings* series gained attention by all ages. This trend continues today with J.K. Rowling's *Harry Potter* series.

Science fiction, a subgenre of fantasy, has grown in popularity through the years. While science fiction also occurs in an imaginary world, its plot and characters deal with the impact of science and technology on humans and their daily existence. The genre of science fiction began in 1818 with Shelley's *Frankenstein* and grew in popularity through Jules Verne's *Journey to the Center of the Earth* in 1870 and H.G. Wells's *The War of the Worlds* in 1898. While science fiction novels frequently involve aliens and outer space themes, they can also take place in a futuristic society on earth, as evidenced in Lowry's *The Giver* and Orwell's *1984.*

In addition to occurring in a futuristic, fantastical society, Lowry's *The Giver* invokes a dystopian world view. The term **dystopia** was first used in 1868 to mean the opposite of More's *Utopia* where everything was perfect and everyone was personally fulfilled. Dystopian societies in literature are often created as ideal societies, but evolve into a dangerous place when the community's structure and rules are taken too far. As in many dystopian novels, the community in *The Giver* places strict restrictions on the characters' lives and does not tolerate individual thoughts or actions. The novel's conflict, as in many dystopian novels, revolves around the main character's feelings that something is wrong in his community, and how he reconciles his feelings living within such a structured society. By incorporating a dystopian society into *The Giver*, Lowry draws on the literary traditions of Huxley's *Brave New World* and Bradbury's *Fahrenheit 451.*

By the use of technology in a fantasy world gone wrong, Lois Lowry firmly places *The Giver* in the dystopian tradition of classic science fiction and fantasy novels.

Name ____ Period ____________

Standards Focus: Exploring Expository Writing—Genre

Directions*: After reading the article about genres on page 11, answer the following questions. Write the letter of the correct answer on the line.*

1. ________What aspect of traditional fantasy novels does Lowry utilize in *The Giver*?
   a. a recognizable setting
   b. a plot centered on science and technology
   c. setting the novel in a "lost world"
   d. basing the plot on historical events

2. ________Which of the following novels is not an example of science fiction?
   a. *Journey to the Center of the Earth*
   b. *Wizard of Oz*
   c. *Frankenstein*
   d. *War of the Worlds*

3. ________Which of the following is NOT a characteristic of a dystopian novel?
   a. It occurs in a supposedly perfect society which has gone too far.
   b. The main character must try to reconcile his/her individuality to the structure of the society in which he/she lives.
   c. The novel occurs in a realistic setting.
   d. The characters' lives and individuality are restricted.

4. ________Which of the following most closely describes the opinion of the author of the article on page 11 regarding science fiction?
   a. The author does not enjoy reading science fiction.
   b. Science fiction is the author's favorite genre to read.
   c. The author believes that science fiction helps assess the role that technology plays in our lives.
   d. The author does not state his/her opinion of science fiction.

5. Explain the difference between a utopian and a dystopian society. ______________

____

____

____

6. How are the genres of fantasy and science fiction related? Explain the differences and similarities between them. ______________________________________

____

____

____

____

Name ____ Period ____________

Standards Focus: Allusions and Terminology

<u>Chapter One</u>

- **landing field**- runway where airplanes land
- **needle-nosed single-pilot jet**- small, fast airplane with one pilot and no passengers
- **hymn**- song of praise
- **hatchery**- place for hatching fish eggs
- **salmon**- a type of fish which is frequently eaten as food
- **tunic**- a long shirt
- **port**- a specific place where a vehicle is parked
- **rituals**- social customs which are done repeatedly
- **learning usages**- ways of doing things
- **Nurturer**- a person assigned to care for infants
- **newchild**- infant
- **gender**- male or female sex
- **spouses**- husbands or wives
- **Department of Justice**- court and legal systems

<u>Chapter Two</u>

- **Elders**- an official position of rank and authority
- **appeal process**- legal proceedings in which a person requests that a decision or ruling be changed
- **comfort object**- an item, typically a stuffed animal, that a child uses to console himself

<u>Chapter Three</u>

- **Birthmother**- biological mother
- **singsong voice**- speaking in a rhythmic, lilting tone
- **sphere**- three-dimensional circle, like a ball
- **dwelling**- house
- **magnifying glass**- handheld object used to make items appear larger

<u>Chapter Four</u>

- **bikeports**- parking places for bicycles; a bike rack
- **groupmates**- class of children who are the same age
- **community structures**- public buildings
- **House of the Old**- home for elderly people, similar to a nursing home
- **attendant**- a person who greets visitors; a secretary
- **Caretaker**- a person assigned to work with the elderly
- **family unit**- group of people consisting of a mother, father, and one or two children who live together

<u>Chapter Five</u>

- **Security Guards**- police officers
- **Stirrings**- feelings of sexual desire

<u>Chapter Six</u>

- **Assignment**- job which a person is given
- **Auditorium**- public building for large gatherings of people
- **Naming and Placement**- ceremony in which a child is given a name and placed in a family

Name ____ Period ____________

- **Inadequate**- a child who does not meet the developmental standards for his/her age
- **Uncertain**- a child whose developmental status is not yet determined
- **Ceremony of Loss**- funeral service for a person who dies accidentally or prematurely
- **Murmur-of-Replacement Ceremony**- service in which a name is reintroduced to the community
- **podium**- stand on which a speaker places his/her notes
- **midday meal**- lunch
- **Sanitation Laborer**- person who picks up trash
- **Matching of Spouses**- process of selecting males and females to create a family unit
- **Committee of Elders**- group of authority figures who make decisions about the community

Chapter Seven
- **tattletale**- informing an authority figure when someone does something wrong
- **precision of language**- using specific vocabulary words to fit a situation

Chapter Eight
- **crescendo**- increase in volume of music
- **integrity**- adhering to moral values
- **courage**- mental strength to overcome danger and fear
- **wisdom**- knowledge

Chapter Nine
- **carrying containers**- box or basket for storage on the back of a bicycle
- **Nurturing Center**- facility where infants are cared for until they are placed in a family unit
- **Not-to-Be-Spoken**- name which is not to be used or person who is not to be referred to
- **sleepingroom**- bedroom
- **Twelve**- a twelve-year-old child; the age when a person is assigned a job
- **Four**- a four-year-old child

Chapter Ten
- **citizen-in-training**- a twelve-year-old child who is learning to do the job which he/she was assigned

Chapter Eleven
- **Annex-** a separate room attached to a larger building
- **Sameness**- all persons and items appearing and acting alike, as well as experiencing the same things
- **Climate Control**- managing the weather so that it is always the same
- **transmission**- the process of one person giving a memory to another person

Chapter Twelve
- **discipline wand**- small stick-like instrument used to strike a person who misbehaves
- **occupational therapy**- exercises which promote recovery or rehabilitation
- **seeing beyond**- the ability to perceive qualities, such as colors, which are not viewed by others
- **one-generation memories**- recollections of personal experiences
- **"work the kinks out"**- fix the problems

Name ____ Period ____________

Chapter Thirteen

- **small-muscle control**- using the hand muscles to manipulate objects
- **geraniums**- red flowers with a long stem and round buds
- **Hall of Open Records**- public building where legal documents are stored
- **Landscape Workers**- people who plant and care for natural surroundings such as lawns and flowers

Chapter Fourteen

- **relief-of-pain**- medicine which alleviates bodily discomforts
- **anesthetic ointment**- numbing medicine which is rubbed on the skin
- **spasms**- involuntary muscle contractions
- **turquoise**- bluish-green color

Chapter Fifteen

- **whinnying**- horse's neigh

Chapter Sixteen

- **"get his bearings"**- figure out where one is located
- **wholeheartedly**- completely

Chapter Seventeen

- **ambush**- attacking a person or group by surprise
- **counter-attack**- to fight against a person or group

Chapter Nineteen

- **syringe**- a device used to inject fluids; a shot
- **plunger**- a device which forces liquid out of a syringe

Chapter Twenty-One

- **frazzled**- nervously upset; anxious
- **fugitives**- persons who are trying to escape from the police

Chapter Twenty-Two

- **perils**- dangers
- **banquets**- meals with large displays of items to eat

Name ______________________________ Period __________

Vocabulary List

***Directions**: Use a dictionary or the author's words to find the meanings of the following words from The Giver. Your teacher will direct you to do this lesson either as you read each chapter or as a pre-reading activity. Whatever method your teacher chooses, be sure to keep this list and your definitions to use in vocabulary exercises and to study for quizzes and tests.*

Chapters One-Two
1. ironic (2)
2. palpable (3)
3. wheedle (5)
4. disposition (7)
5. transgression (9)
6. awed (12)
7. technically (13)
8. aptitude (15)

Chapters Three-Four
1. chastise (20)
2. petulantly (22)
3. remorse (23)
4. conviction (24)
5. hasten (27)
6. tabulated (28)
7. nuisance (30)
8. chortled (33)

Chapters Five-Six
1. disquieting (34)
2. emblem (41)
3. reprieve (42)
4. relinquish (42)
5. exuberant (44)
6. infringed (46)
7. meticulously (48)
8. scrupulously (48)

Chapters Seven-Eight
1. profound (51)
2. prestige (53)
3. retroactive (54)
4. avert (57)
5. benign (59)
6. indolence (61)
7. unanimous (61)
8. spontaneously (64)

Chapters Nine-Ten
1. throng (65)
2. dismounting (66)
3. relish (68)
4. integral (70)
5. origin (73)
6. alcove (74)
7. successor (76)
8. apprehensively (79)

Chapters Eleven-Twelve
1. torrent (81)
2. glee (82)
3. obsolete (84)
4. wincing (86)
5. commerce (89)
6. admonition (89)
7. dumbfounded (93)
8. wryly (95)

Chapters Thirteen-Fourteen
1. irrationally (99)
2. sinuous (100)
3. assimilated (104)
4. embedded (106)
5. agony (109)
6. assuage (110)
7. ominous (113)
8. placidly (114)

Chapters Fifteen-Seventeen
1. anguish (118)
2. ecstatic (122)
3. wisp (125)
4. permeated (131)
5. injustice (132)
6. expertise (134)
7. trudged (135)
8. glum (136)

Chapters Eighteen-Twenty
1. dejected (139)
2. excruciating (140)
3. inflict (142)
4. afterthought (146)
5. wretched (151)
6. empowered (153)
7. acquire (156)
8. solace (161)

Chapters Twenty-One-Twenty-Three
1. churning (163)
2. rueful (164)
3. languid (166)
4. augmented (168)
5. vigilant (169)
6. tantalizing (172)
7. impeded (176)
8. leaden (177)

Name ____________________ Period __________

Anticipation/Reaction Guide

***Directions**: For the following statements and questions, compose a well-written sentence giving your reaction or answer to each. Do you agree? Disagree? Why?*

1. *Euthanasia* is the practice of medically ending a person's life when he/she has become hopelessly sick or injured without any chance of recovery.
   a. People should be euthanized when they are very sick, elderly, or no longer useful to society. ____________________
   ____
   ____
   b. If human euthanasia was common, who should decide when a person is euthanized? Why? ____________________
   ____
   ____
   c. Do you think it should be all right for a person to request to be euthanized? Why or why not? ____________________
   ____
   ____
   d. In our society, sick pets are commonly euthanized. Why is it viewed as acceptable to euthanize a sick pet, but not an ill person? ____________________
   ____
   ____
2. In America, we are constitutionally given *freedom of choice*. However, there are laws that limit these choices, i.e. we do not have the freedom to choose to kill someone (without punishment), and until the age of 18, you do not legally have the right to make your own choices; your parents have this right for you.
   a. It would be better to have complete freedom of choice, even if people sometimes made poor choices. ____________________
   ____
   ____
   b. In what situations might it be best for someone to make your choices for you? Why?
   ____
   ____
   ____

Name ____ Period ___________

c. What choices should you have the option to make on your own? (i.e. choice of spouse, having children, choice of career, whether or not to attend college) ______________

____

____

3. By definition, a *utopia* is an ideal and perfect society in which everyone lives in harmony and everything is done for the good of its citizens.

a. Describe what a "perfect" society means to you. ______________________

____

____

b. I would rather live in a "perfect" society than in a flawed one. _______________

____

____

____

c. Who should be in charge of the "perfect" society? ______________________

____

____

d. Name some aspects of our society which are flawed and could be improved. (i.e. more affordable health care, crime rate) ______________________________

____

____

4. An *ordered* society is one with rules and consequences for breaking those rules. A *chaotic* society is freer, without order or law, and without consequences.

a. Would you categorize our society as ordered or chaotic? Why? ______________

____

____

b. What would be an advantage/disadvantage of living in an ordered society without family and loving relationships?______________________________

____

____

c. What would be an advantage/disadvantage of living in a chaotic society with family and loving relationships?

____

____

____

Name ____ Period ___________

Anticipation/Reaction Guide Reflection

***Directions**: After the entire class has had time to discuss their responses to pages 17-18, form small groups to discuss the class's answers as well as your small group members' answers. Listen carefully to their responses, paying attention to your classmates' opinions. After you have discussed your responses, answer the following questions on the lines below. Your answers should be well thought out and provide thorough answers to the questions.*

1. Which statement triggered the most thought-provoking or interesting discussion among the class or your group members? ______________________________
____

2. Summarize the discussion. ______________________________________
____
____
____
____
____

3. For any statements that you discussed, what were some of the strongest or most important points made by your group members? ________________________
____
____
____
____
____

4. How did those arguments affect your opinion? Was any argument strong enough to make you change your mind or want to change any of your initial responses? Why or why not? What made you want to change your mind? ____________________
____
____
____
____
____
____

Name ____ Period ____________

Active Reading Guide: Note-Taking and Summarizing

To help you keep track of the novel's events as they occur, you will be keeping notes using a chart similar to the one below. For each chapter, fill in the chart with the necessary information. Directions for how to complete the chart are in the boxes below. *See page 21 for an example using Chapter One.*

Setting	*(Write a description of where the action occurs, including approximate time period.)*
Characters	*(List and describe important information about the characters in the chapter.)* 1. 2. 3. 4. 5. 6.
Summary of the Chapter	*(Write a 3-5 sentence summary of the chapter.)*
Prediction of Coming Events	*(Make a prediction of what you think will occur in the next chapter.)*

Name ____ Period ____________

Chapters One—Two

Sample Note-Taking and Summarizing: Chapter 1

To help you keep track of the novel's events as they happen, you will be keeping notes using a chart similar to the one below to help summarize the important details for each chapter. ***Directions:*** *For each chapter, fill in the chart with the necessary information. An example for Chapter One is below. (Note: You do not need to write in complete sentences.)*

Setting	*(A description of where the action occurs.)* The novel begins in December in an unnamed community sometime in the future. After beginning outdoors, the scene progresses to the interior of Jonas's home.
Characters	*(List and describe important information about the characters in the chapter.)* 1. Jonas- 11-year-old boy who is apprehensive about the upcoming Ceremony of Twelve 2. Lily- Jonas's 7-year-old little sister 3. Asher- Jonas's friend who is frequently reprimanded 4. Jonas's father- works as a Nurturer 5. Jonas's mother- works at the Department of Justice
Summary of the Chapter	*(A 3-5 sentence summary of the chapter.)* Jonas recalls feeling frightened when an unidentified jet flew over his community, and all the citizens were ordered to go inside. At the nightly "telling of feelings," Lily shares her frustration at playing with children who do not understand the rules. Father discusses a baby that he is nurturing at work, and Jonas confides that he is nervous about his upcoming Ceremony of Twelve.
Prediction of Coming Events	*(Make a prediction of what you think will occur next.)* Since Jonas discusses feeling scared and apprehensive, I think that something unexpected and frightening will happen to him.

Name ____ Period ____________

Note-Taking and Summarizing: Chapter 2

Setting	*(Write a description of where the action occurs, including approximate time period.)*
Characters	*(List and describe important information about the characters in the chapter.)* 1. 2. 3. 4. 5. 6.
Summary of the Chapter	*(Write a 3-5 sentence summary of the chapter.)*
Prediction of Coming Events	*(Make a prediction of what you think will occur in the next chapter.)*

Name ______________________________________ Period __________

Chapters One—Two
Comprehension Check

Directions: *To help you understand all aspects of the novel, answer the following questions for Chapters 1-2. Write your answers on a separate piece of paper using complete sentences.*

Chapter One

1. Explain why you think airplanes are not permitted to fly over the community.
2. List the different jobs that are mentioned in the chapter.
3. Discuss how the citizens and the Pilot are treated during the accidental fly-over.
4. Examine how Asher apologizes to his classmates when he is late to class. Do you think he should have to apologize in this way?
5. Several rituals, such as using a standard apology phrase and the nightly sharing of feelings, are described. Generalize why these rituals are used in the community.
6. What are Elevens and Sevens?
7. Compare your family's nightly routine to Jonas's family's nightly rituals.
8. Distinguish Lily's definition of animals from our definition of them. Why do you think Lily's definition might be different from ours?
9. Compare Father's job as Nurturer to a similar job in our society.
10. Explain why the male baby that Father discusses may be released.
11. Identify three reasons why someone may be released.
12. How are family units with parents and children created?
13. Why does Jonas's family share their feelings at dinner each evening? Why do you think this is an important aspect of life in this community? Is this something that is important to your family? Why or why not?

Chapter Two

1. Contrast why December is eventful in Jonas's society with why December is eventful in our society.
2. Describe and assess the Ceremony for the Ones. Do you agree or disagree with the community's way of handling birthdays? How?
3. Explain how babies are placed with families. What do you think about this arrangement? Do you think it is good or bad for the children? Explain your response.
4. Analyze where and how newchildren live until they are one. How could this affect their development?
5. Show how Father attempts to enhance Gabriel's nurturing.
6. Which rule is frequently broken?
7. How are rules changed in the community? How frequently does this occur?
8. Who is the most important Elder?
9. Explain how and when Assignments are made.
10. What do you think would happen if a citizen did not want to do his/her Assignment? What Assignment do you think you would be given?
11. Why do you think that individual birthdays are not celebrated? Why is age not important after becoming a Twelve?
12. Decide when and where the novel occurs. Could a society like this one actually be created? Explain your position.

Name ______________________________________ Period ___________

Chapters One—Two
Standards Focus: Foreshadowing

An author frequently includes subtle details or clues which hint at, or **foreshadow**, upcoming events in a novel. Foreshadowing allows an author to build a novel while laying the groundwork for upcoming character and plot development. To utilize foreshadowing, an author must plan the entire scope of a novel before he/she begins to write. Detailed planning allows the author to include foreshadowing throughout the novel.

Directions*: Below are some examples of foreshadowing in* <u>The Giver</u>*. For each example, write a* ***specific prediction*** *about the character or plot development that you believe is being foreshadowed. After you finish reading the novel, reread your predictions to see how accurate they were. An example has been done for you.*

Ex. Frightened meant that deep, sickening feeling of something terrible about to happen. Frightened was the way he had felt a year ago when an unidentified aircraft had overflown the community twice. . . . He had never seen aircraft so close, for it was against the rules for Pilots to fly over the community. (pg. 1)

Prediction: <u>Planes flying over the community will frighten Jonas in the future. They may be war planes about to attack the community.</u>

1. Father was listening with interest. "I'm thinking, Lily," he said, "about the boy who didn't obey the rules today. Do you think it's possible that he felt strange and stupid, being in a new place with rules that he didn't know about?"

   Lily pondered that. "Yes," she said, finally.

   "I feel a little sorry for him," Jonas said, "even though I don't even know him. I feel sorry for anyone who is in a place where he feels strange and stupid." (pg. 6)

   Prediction: ____

   ____

   ____

2. Jonas and Lily nodded sympathetically as well. Release of newchildren was always sad, because they hadn't had a chance to enjoy life within the community yet. And they hadn't done anything wrong.

   There were only two occasions of release which were not punishment. Release of the elderly, which was a time of celebration for a life well and fully lived; and release of a newchild, which always brought a sense of what-could-we-have-done. This was especially troubling for the Nurturers, like Father, who felt they had failed somehow. But it happened very rarely. (pgs. 7-8)

Name ____ Period ____________

Prediction: ____

____

____

3. Jonas shivered. He knew it happened. There was even a boy in his group of Elevens whose father had been released years before. No one ever mentioned it; the disgrace was unspeakable. (pg. 9)

Prediction: ____

____

____

4. His father nodded. "His name—if he makes it to the Naming without being released, of course—is to be Gabriel. So I whisper that to him when I feed him every four hours, and during exercise and playtime." (pg. 12)

Prediction: ____

____

____

5. The Receiver was the most important Elder. Jonas had never even seen him, that he knew of; someone in a position of such importance lived and worked alone. (pg. 14)

Prediction: ____

____

____

6. "But it means," his mother went on, "that you'll move into a new group. And each of your friends will. You'll no longer be spending your time with your group of Elevens. After the Ceremony of Twelve, you'll be with your Assignment group, with those in training. No more volunteer hours. No more recreation hours. So your friends will no longer be as close." (pgs. 17-18)

Prediction: ____

____

____

7. Though he had been reassured by the talk with his parents, he hadn't the slightest idea what Assignment the Elders would be selecting for his future, or how he might feel about it when the day came. (pg. 19)

Prediction: ____

____

____

Name ____ Period ____________

Chapters One—Two
Assessment Preparation: Punctuation, Capitalization, Spelling, and Grammar

***Directions**: Find the errors in punctuation, capitalization, spelling, and grammar for each of the following sentences. Rewrite the sentences, correcting the errors you find. There is more than one error for each sentence. An example has been done for you.*

Ex. I'd been teaching her to ride mine even though technicaly I weren't supposed to.

I'd been teaching her to ride mine, even though technically I wasn't supposed to.

1. There was a ironic tone to that final mesage, as if the Speaker found it amusing and jonas had smiled a little, though he knew what a grim statement it has been.

____

____

____

2. now, thinking about the feeling of fear as he pedaled home along the river path, he remembers that moment of palpable stomach-sinking terror when the aircraft had streked above.

____

____

____

3. "Mail, father said. Hes a sweet little mail with a lovely disposition."

____

4. "i feel frightened, to, for him" she confessed. "You know that there's not no third chance. The rules say that if there's a third transgression, he simply has to be released.

____

____

____

Name ____ Period ____________

5. It didn't seem a terrible important rule, but the fact that his father had broke a rule at all awed him

____

____

6. "All the things I do with my friends" jonas pointed out, and his mother nodded in agrement.

____

____

7. For a contributing citizen to be released from the community was a final decision, a terrible punishment, an overwhelming statement of failure

____

____

8. I apologize for inconveniencing my learning community." asher ran through the standard apology phrase rapidly, still catching his breath.

____

____

____

9. "Why do you think the visitors didn't obey the rules" mother asked.

____

____

10. "I'm feeling apprehensive," He confesed, "glad that the appropriate descriptive word has finally came to him."

____

____

____

Name ______________________________________ Period ____________

Chapters Three—Four
Note-Taking and Summarizing: Chapter 3

Setting	
Characters	
Summary of the Chapter	
Prediction of Coming Events	

Name ____ Period ____________

Note-Taking and Summarizing: Chapter 4

Setting	
Characters	
Summary of the Chapter	
Prediction of Coming Events	

Name ____ Period ___________

Chapters Three—Four
Comprehension Check

Directions: *To help you understand all aspects of the novel, answer the following questions for Chapters 3-4. Write your answers on a separate piece of paper using complete sentences.*

Chapter Three

1. Infer why citizens are only allowed to use bicycles for individual transportation. What implications does this have for travel?
2. What physical trait do Jonas and Gabriel share?
3. Examine how this trait could link Jonas and Gabriel.
4. Summarize how Birthmothers are regarded in the community.
5. Generalize how individual differences and appearances are treated in the community.
6. Explain why Birthmothers never see newchildren.
7. Tell why Jonas takes the apple home.
8. Explain why Asher has to play catch.
9. Prepare a schedule for Jonas's family to follow when caring for Gabriel at night.
10. Differentiate most American families' evening routines from families' nightly routines in the community.

Chapter Four

1. Apply your knowledge of the community to explain why Assignments and the loss of free time occur at a young age.
2. What does the statement *The rule against bragging is a good idea that is taken too far in the community* mean? Do you agree or disagree? Why?
3. List items which are provided for members of the community.
4. How are the Ceremony of Twelve and Release of the Elderly celebrated as the only times a citizen is singled out as an individual?
5. Predict what Jonas's Assignment will be and why he receives that Assignment.
6. Illustrate how newchildren and the elderly are treated similarly.
7. Plan a Release Ceremony for an elderly person with whom you are acquainted. To where would you release him or her?

Name ____ Period ____________

Chapters Three—Four
Standards Focus: Point of View

Point of view is the viewpoint, or perspective, from which a story is told. The point of view influences how a reader understands a story and how he reacts to the characters and their actions.

A novel may be told from the point of view of one of the book's characters or from the point of view of a narrator who is not part of the novel.

Even though *The Giver* is not written in first person with Jonas using the pronoun "I" to refer to himself, the novel is written from Jonas's point of view and focuses on his thoughts and feelings. This point of view is called *Third Person Limited.*

Directions: *Use your knowledge of the novel to answer the following questions in complete sentences. Include specific details from the text in your answers.*

1. From Jonas's point of view, Lily is too talkative. What comments from Chapters 3-4 does Jonas make that allows the reader to draw this conclusion?

____

____

____

2. Read the following passage:

    "'Three years,' Mother told her firmly. 'Three births, and that's all. After that they are Laborers for the rest of their adult lives, until the day that they enter the House of the Old. Is that what you want, Lily? Three lazy years, and then hard physical labor until you are old?'" (pg.22)

    It is obvious that Mother does not value the Assignment of Birthmother. How do you think a Birthmother feels about her Assignment? Would she think it is or is not important? Why or why not?

____

____

____

3. Read the following passage:

    "There was absolutely nothing remarkable about that apple. He had tossed it back and forth between his hands a few times, then thrown it again to Asher. And again—in the air, for an instant only—it had changed.

    Jonas had been completely mystified.

    'Ash?' he had called. 'Does anything seem strange to you? About the apple?'

Name ____ Period ___________

'Yes,' Asher called back, laughing. 'It jumps out of my hand onto the ground!' Asher had just dropped it once again." (pg. 24)

While playing catch with Asher, Jonas notices something different about an apple and later takes it home. A) What was Jonas's reason for taking it home? From Jonas's point of view his actions were justified, but Asher probably saw Jonas's actions as strange. B) Think about situation in which you felt your words and/or actions were appropriate for the situation, but others did not. Write about the situation.

A)____

B)____

____

____

____

4. Read the following passage:

"It was against the rules for children or adults to look at another's nakedness; but the rule did not apply to newchildren or the Old. Jonas was glad. It was a nuisance to keep oneself covered while changing for games, and the required apology if one had by mistake glimpsed another's body was always awkward. He couldn't see why it was necessary. He liked the feeling of safety here in this warm and quiet room; he liked the expression of trust on the woman's face as she lay in the water unprotected, exposed, and free." (pg. 30)

Jonas enjoys being in the bathing room at the House of the Old because he views it as relaxing and safe. Since the story is basically told from Jonas's point of view, we can only speculate about the feelings of some of the other characters. How do you think Larissa feels about being bathed by Jonas? Do you think she feels safe? Why or why not?

____

____

____

____

5. Since *The Giver* is written from the point of view of a citizen of the community, the community's rules and rituals are presented as a normal part of life. If you visited the community, what would you think of the community's rules and rituals? Which ones would you find particularly odd?

____

____

____

____

____

Name ____ Period ____________

Assessment Preparation: Word Origins—Etymology

Directions: *For each of the vocabulary words from Chapters 3-4:*

a. Read the origin of the word.
b. Draw an inference of the vocabulary word's meaning based upon the word's origin.
c. Look up the actual meaning in a dictionary.
d. Write a sentence using the vocabulary word with its correct definition.

An example has been done for you.

Ex. chastise

a. Word Origin: from Latin *castigare* "to drive"

b. My Definition: to drive away wrongdoing

c. Dictionary Definition: to correct or punish

d. Sentence: The boy's father will chastise him for speaking rudely to his mother.

1. petulant

a. Word Origin: from Latin *petere* "to go to, attack, seek"

b. My Definition: ____

c. Dictionary Definition: ______________________________________

____

d. Sentence: ____

____

2. remorse

a. Word Origin: from Latin *remordere* "to bite again"

b. My Definition: ____

c. Dictionary Definition: ______________________________________

____

d. Sentence: ____

____

3. conviction

a. Word Origin: from Latin *convincere* "to refute; convict"

b. My Definition: ____

c. Dictionary Definition: ______________________________________

____

Name ______________________________ Period __________

d. Sentence: ______________________________

____

4. hasten

a. Word Origin: from Old English *haest* "violence"

b. My Definition: ______________________________

c. Dictionary Definition: ______________________________

____

d. Sentence: ______________________________

____

5. tabulate

a. Word Origin: from Latin *tabula* "tablet"

b. My Definition: ______________________________

c. Dictionary Definition: ______________________________

____

d. Sentence: ______________________________

____

6. nuisance

a. Word Origin: from Old French *nuisir* "to harm"

b. My Definition: ______________________________

c. Dictionary Definition: ______________________________

____

d. Sentence: ______________________________

____

7. chortle

a. Word Origin: unknown; probably a blend of *chuckle* and *snort*

b. My Definition: ______________________________

c. Dictionary Definition: ______________________________

____

d. Sentence: ______________________________

____

Name ____ Period ____________

Chapters Five—Six
Note-Taking and Summarizing: Chapter 5

Setting	
Characters	
Summary of the Chapter	
Prediction of Coming Events	

Name ____ Period ____________

Note-Taking and Summarizing: Chapter 6

Setting	
Characters	
Summary of the Chapter	
Prediction of Coming Events	

Name ____ Period ____________

Chapters Five–Six
Comprehension Check

Directions: *To help you understand all aspects of the novel, answer the following questions for Chapters 5-6. Write your answers on a separate piece of paper using complete sentences.*

Chapter Five

1. What do you think is the true purpose of the daily telling of dreams?
2. Discuss how Lily's and Mother's dreams reveal their feelings about the community's structure.
3. Examine the role of mothers in the community. Do you think the mothers have the option of deciding whether to stay home with their children or go to work? Why or why not?
4. Generalize why both parents in the family unit work outside the home and why the family includes only non-biological children.
5. What does Jonas's dream reveal about his psychological and physical development?
6. Contrast Jonas's actual experience bathing Larissa with his dream involving Fiona.
7. Explain how you would feel if you had to report all of your dreams and feelings to your family and the government.
8. Analyze the effects the pills have on the citizens.
9. Formulate why the community Elders would not want the citizens to have Stirrings.
10. Tell how Jonas feels about no longer experiencing Stirrings.

Chapter Six

1. Name the major annual celebration in the community.
2. Show how the concept of "grouping" dominates the community.
3. Recommend a change to one of the age groupings. Justify your recommendation with reasons based on the text.
4. Assess whether Gabriel would develop better at the Nurturing Center for another year or with a name and a family. Provide reasons to support your answer.
5. Describe the Ceremony of Loss and the Murmur-of-Replacement Ceremony.
6. Explain the irony of each person having a name that no other individual in this particular community has.
7. Compare and contrast Jonas's neighborhood with yours.
8. Hypothesize what occurs when a citizen applies for Elsewhere.
9. Illustrate, in paragraph form, your vision of Elsewhere.
10. Create a situation in which someone may not fit into the community regardless of the "meticulous" and careful choices of the community's Elders.
11. How does Jonas show total trust in the Elders' decisions? Why do you think he is so trusting?

Name ____ Period ____________

Chapters Five–Six
Standards Focus: Symbolism

In literature, authors frequently use **symbols** to demonstrate meanings in a story. Just as blooming flowers represent spring and changing leaves illustrate fall, an author utilizes **symbolism** to add depth to his/her writing. In *The Giver*, Lois Lowry connects each year of a child's life with a different symbol to represent his/her changing status in the community.

Directions: *List the changes that each child experiences by year given in Chapters One-Six. Also indicate what each change symbolizes for the child's growth and maturity. Once you have completed the chart below, complete the chart on page 39.*

Age	Changes	Symbolism
Ones		
Fours-Sixes	Jacket that buttons in the back	
Sevens		
Eights		
Nines		
Tens		
Elevens		
Twelves		No longer a child, but a contributing member of the community

In the novel, Gabriel is becoming a part of Jonas's family unit. In the Bible, Gabriel is the angel who predicted Jesus's birth. What clue may this give the reader about Gabriel's role in *The Giver?*

____

____

Name ____ Period __________

____

____

____

Even in our society, we have rituals and events that mark important milestones of life. Complete the chart below with examples of changes, and the symbolism of these events, that are important within our society.

Age	**Changes**	**Symbolism**
Birth		
Four or Five		
Thirteen		
Fifteen or Sixteen		
Eighteen		
Twenty-One		

What is your impression of the difference in milestones in Jonas's society and ours? Explain the drawbacks and benefits of each.

____

____

____

____

____

____

____

____

Name ____ Period ____________

Chapters Five–Six
Assessment Preparation: Identifying Parts of Speech

To understand how the English language is constructed, it is necessary to learn and recognize the **parts of speech**. If a sentence does not make sense, it may be missing a particular part of speech, or a part of speech may be used incorrectly. There are eight main parts of speech: nouns, verbs, adjectives, adverbs, conjunctions, pronouns, interjections, and prepositions.

Directions: *For each of the following sentences, determine the part of speech for each of the underlined words in the sentence. Write the part of speech on the line provided.*

1. Jonas said the standard phrase automatically (*a*), and tried to pay better attention while his mother told of a dream fragment, a disquieting (*b*) scene where she had been chastised (*c*) for a rule infraction she didn't understand.

   a. ________________ b. ____________________ c. ________________

2. The bicycle, at Nine, would be the (*a*) powerful emblem (*b*) of moving gradually out (*c*) into the community, away from the protective family unit.

   a. ________________ b. ____________________ c. ________________

3. He had been given an unusual and special reprieve (*a*) from the committee, and (*b*) granted an additional year of nurturing (*c*) before his Naming and Placement.

   a. ________________ b. ____________________ c. ________________

4. Each (*a*) family member was required to sign a pledge that they would relinquish (*b*) him without protest or appeal when he (*c*) was assigned to his own family unit at next year's Ceremony.

   a. ________________ b. ____________________ c. ________________

Name ____ Period ____________

a *b*

5. The audience applause, which was enthusiastic at each Naming, rose in an exuberant
c
swell when one parental pair, glowing with pride, took a male newchild and heard him named Caleb.

a. _______________ b. __________________ c. _______________

a *b*

6. But each such error reflected negatively on his parents' guidance and infringed on the
c
community's sense of order and success.

a. _______________ b. __________________ c. _______________

a *b* *c*

7. The community was so meticulously ordered, the choices so carefully made.

a. _______________ b. __________________ c. _______________

a

8. Like the Matching of Spouses and the Naming and Placement of newchildren, the
b *c*
Assignments were scrupulously thought through by the Committee of Elders.

a. _______________ b. __________________ c. _______________

a *b* *c*

9. He watched while Mother tidied the remains of the morning meal and placed the tray
d
by the front door for the Collection Crew.

a. _______________ b. __________________

c. _______________ d. __________________

a *b*

10. He sat politely through the ceremonies of Two and Three and Four, increasingly
c *d*
bored as he was each year.

a. _______________ b. __________________

c. _______________ d. __________________

Name ______________________________ Period __________

Chapters Seven—Eight

Note-Taking and Summarizing: Chapter 7

Setting	
Characters	
Summary of the Chapter	
Prediction of Coming Events	

Name ____ Period ____________

Note-Taking and Summarizing: Chapter 8

Setting	
Characters	
Summary of the Chapter	
Prediction of Coming Events	

Name ______________________________________ Period ___________

Chapters Seven—Eight
Comprehension Check

Directions: *To help you understand all aspects of the novel, answer the following questions for Chapters 7-8. Write your answers on a separate piece of paper using complete sentences.*

Chapter 7

1. Explain how the newchildren are identified before they are named.
2. Tell how the Chief Elder is determined.
3. Summarize the behavioral goals of the Elevens and the younger children.
4. Examine the character of Fiona and her abilities.
5. Analyze how many students are assigned to each job per year, and how this ensures a steady flow of workers for the community.
6. Articulate why using precise language is important to the community.
7. Explain how Asher was disciplined for using the incorrect word for "snack." Assess whether he received an appropriate or inappropriate consequence for misusing a word. Provide reasons to support your answer.
8. What is Asher's Assignment? How does his Assignment affirm the Committee's choice of Assignments?
9. Describe what occurs as Jonas waits to be called to the stage.
10. Explain what Jonas thinks when his number is skipped.

Chapter 8

1. Describe the applause when Jonas is finally called to the stage.
2. "Discomfort" is frequently used to describe the community's feelings. Why are the citizens uncomfortable? What adjectives may more precisely describe the community's feelings?
3. Contrast how Jonas anticipated he would approach the stage with how he actually does so.
4. Write a description of the Receiver.
5. Explain why the community could not afford another failure with the Receiver-in-Training.
6. List the rules which govern the Receiver-in-Training.
7. List and explain the five qualities the Receiver must possess.
8. Explain Jonas's reaction to Seeing Beyond.
9. Based on what you know about the Receiver, would you want this Assignment? Provide reasons to support your answer.
10. How does Jonas feel about becoming the Receiver-in-Training?

Name ____ Period ____________

Chapters Seven—Eight
Standards Focus: Setting and Problem

Setting is one of the most important aspects of a novel. **Setting** includes:

- Time: historical time period, season, time of day
- Geographical location: weather, landforms, physical arrangement of locations
- General Environment: religious, mental, moral, and emotional conditions
- Social/Political Environment: daily manner of living, occupations, rules and government

Problem is the conflict that occurs in a novel. A desire to see the problem resolved encourages the reader to keep reading a book. In *The Giver*, the novel's setting contributes to the conflicts and problems that occur.

***Directions**: For each section, answer the questions about the novel's setting in complete sentences. Think about how the setting creates conflicts in the novel.*

Time

1. When does the novel take place? ______________________________________
____
2. What season or time of year is it? ____________________________________
____
3. Without seasons, how does the community keep time? ____________________
____

Geography

4. What types of weather occur in the community? __________________________
____
5. What types of landforms, such as hills and rivers, exist in the community? _____
____
6. Describe the homes and buildings in the community. ______________________
____
____
7. How does the Sameness in the community's geography parallel the community's structures and values? ____
____
____

Name ____ Period _____________

General Environment

8. Explain the community's religious and moral beliefs. ______________________
____
____
____

9. Explain how individual thought and personal decision-making is stifled in this community. ____
____
____

10. What problems might be created in a society that puts the needs of the community above all personal/individual desires? _________________________________
____
____
____
____

Social/Political Environment

11. How do citizens select a career? How do Assignments complement the community's goals? ____
____
____
____

12. What aspects of citizens' daily lives does the government control? ____________
____
____
____

13. What problems might occur because of this? ____________________________
____
____
____
____

Name ____ Period ____________

Chapters Seven–Eight
Assessment Preparation: Vocabulary in Context

When reading, you must infer the meaning of words by looking at **context clues**. Context clues are words located in a sentence or paragraph that help the reader figure out the meaning of unfamiliar vocabulary. In addition to looking for context clues, a reader must also look at how the word is used in the sentence to infer its meaning.

Directions: *For each vocabulary word (in* **bold** *print), first indicate the part of speech in which the word appears (noun, verb, etc.). Also, infer an original definition for the vocabulary word based upon the clues in the sentence. Finally, look up the word and write its definition.*

Ex. The speech was much the same each year: recollection of the time of childhood and the period of preparation, the coming responsibilities of adult life, the **profound** importance of Assignment, the seriousness of training to come.

a. Part of Speech: adjective

b. Inference: deep, strong

c. Definition: great, deep, strong, or intense

1. Birthmother was an important job, if lacking in **prestige**.

   a. Part of Speech: ____

   b. Inference: ____

   c. Definition: ____

   ____

2. "In fact," the Chief Elder continued, chuckling a little herself, "we even gave a little thought to some **retroactive** chastisement for the one who had been Asher's Instructor of Threes so long ago."

   a. Part of Speech: ____

   b. Inference: ____

   c. Definition: ____

   ____

Name ____ Period ____________

3. He saw the others in his group glance at him, embarrassed, and then **avert** their eyes quickly.

   a. Part of Speech: ____

   b. Inference: ____

   c. Definition: ____

   ____

4. The community, relieved from its discomfort very slightly by her **benign** statement, seemed to breathe more easily.

   a. Part of Speech: ____

   b. Inference: ____

   c. Definition: ____

   ____

5. What we observe as playfulness and patience – the requirements to become Nurturer – could, with maturity, be revealed as simply foolishness and **indolence**.

   a. Part of Speech: ____

   b. Inference: ____

   c. Definition: ____

   ____

6. "Therefore the selection must be sound. It must be a **unanimous** choice of the committee. They can have no doubts, however fleeting."

   a. Part of Speech: ____

   b. Inference: ____

   c. Definition: ____

   ____

7. Then she turned and left the stage, left him there alone, standing and facing the crowd, which began **spontaneously** the collective murmur of his name.

   a. Part of Speech: ____

   b. Inference: ____

   c. Definition: ____

   ____

Name ____ Period ____________

Chapters Nine—Ten
Note-Taking and Summarizing: Chapter 9

Setting	
Characters	
Summary of the Chapter	
Prediction of Coming Events	

Name ____ Period ___________

Note-Taking and Summarizing: Chapter 10

Setting	
Characters	
Summary of the Chapter	
Prediction of Coming Events	

Name ____ Period ____________

Chapters Nine—Ten
Comprehension Check

Directions: *To help you understand all aspects of the novel, answer the following questions for Chapters 9-10. Write your answers on a separate piece of paper using complete sentences.*

Chapter Nine

1. Tell how the Assignment of Receiver differs from other Assignments.
2. Describe how Jonas's friends treat him differently after the Assignments are announced. Why do you think they do this?
3. How does Lily plan to apply her knowledge of newchildren through her volunteer hours?
4. Explain what happened to the previous Receiver-in-Training.
5. What honors in our society are similar to the honor Jonas receives?
6. Assess the instructions Jonas receives for his Assignment. How would you react if you received these instructions?
7. Describe how Jonas will spend his time as Receiver-in-Training.
8. Recommend how Jonas should handle the prohibition on dream-telling.
9. Predict reasons that a citizen would apply for release.
10. Discuss how being told he may lie alters Jonas's perception of adults.

Chapter 10

1. Tell how the Attendant shows respect for Jonas.
2. Contrast the Receiver's living space with the other citizens' dwellings.
3. What does Jonas realize when he sees the books at the Receiver's office?
4. How are Jonas and the Receiver physically similar?
5. Relate how Jonas and the Receiver are to work together.
6. What memories does the Receiver possess?
7. Examine how Jonas's discussion with the Receiver changes his perceptions of the world.
8. Explain the metaphor of the snow that The Giver uses to describe how the memories impact him.
9. How does the Receiver transmit a memory to Jonas?

Name ____ Period ____________

Chapters Nine–Ten
Standards Focus: Imagery

In a novel, an author strives for his/her words to create a scene in the reader's mind. To create this **imagery,** an author relies on descriptive and figurative language.

Directions: *Read each of the following passages. After reading each one, close your eyes and try to picture the scene in your mind. Once you have the picture in your mind, answer the questions for each passage, based on your own detailed description of the image you see.*

1. *Jonas hurried through the door and found himself in a comfortably furnished living area. It was not unlike his own family unit's dwelling. Furniture was standard throughout the community: practical, sturdy, the function of each piece clearly defined. A bed for sleeping. A table for eating. A desk for studying.*

   All those things were in this spacious room, though each was slightly different from those in his own dwelling. The fabrics on the upholstered chairs and sofa were slightly thicker and more luxurious; the table legs were not straight like those at home, but slender and curved, with a small carved decoration at the foot. The bed, in an alcove at the far end of the room, was draped with a splendid cloth embroidered over its entire surface with intricate designs.

   But the most conspicuous difference was the books . . . this room's walls were completely covered by bookcases, filled, which reached to the ceiling. There must have been hundreds – perhaps thousands – of books, their titles embossed in shiny letters. (pgs. 73-74)

   What kind of picture is formed in your mind? ______________________________

   ____

   ____

   ____

   Is it somewhere you have been before, or is it a made up place, based upon Lowry's description? Explain. ____

   ____

   ____

   Without reading the passage again and while using specific details, vividly describe the place you pictured in your mind. Your description may include the colors, shapes, and details of the images that you picture in the scene. Try to imitate the descriptiveness and detail with which Lowry writes. Don't be afraid to add details based upon your own thoughts. ________________

   ____

   ____

   ____

   ____

   ____

   ____

Name ______________________________ Period __________

2. *"It's as if . . ." The man paused, seeming to search his mind for the right words of description. "It's like going downhill through deep snow on a sled," he said, finally. "At first it's exhilarating: the speed; the sharp, clear air; but then the snow accumulates, builds up on the runners, and you slow, you have to push hard to keep going, and—"* (pg. 78)

Describe the picture you see in your mind. ______________________________

____

____

____

Is it somewhere you have been before, or is it a made up place, based upon Lowry's description? Explain. ______________________________

____

____

Without reading the passage again and while using specific details, vividly describe the place you pictured in your mind. Your description may include the colors, shapes, and details of the images that you picture in the scene. Try to imitate the descriptiveness and detail with which Lowry writes. Don't be afraid to add details based upon your own thoughts. ______________

____

____

____

____

____

____

What are some of the benefits of using specific details in your writing? How does creating imagery help the reader? Explain. ______________________________

____

____

____

____

Select one of the passages above. Create an illustration of the imagery portrayed by the author on a separate piece of paper. Since the author gives so much detail, your drawings should also be very detailed.

Name ____ Period ____________

Chapters Nine—Ten
Assessment Preparation: Verb Tense and Agreement

A **verb** expresses action or a state of being. When writing, the verb must agree in number with the rest of the sentence. The tense of the verb (past, present, or future) must also make logical sense in the context of the sentence.

Example: Holding the folder she had given him, he **make** his way through the throng, looking for his family unit and for Asher.

Correction: Holding the folder she had given him, he **made** his way through the throng, looking for his family unit and for Asher.

He, the subject of the sentence, is singular, so the verb must also be in the singular form. The action of holding the folder has already occurred in the past, so the verb **made** must also be in the past tense.

Directions: *After reading each sentence below, provide a) the subject of the sentence, b) the correct form of the verb in bold print in the given sentence. [Remember that the verb in bold must agree in number (singular or plural) and in tense (past, present, or future) with the subject in the context of the sentence.] Then in c) rewrite the entire sentence, changing the tense of the entire sentence to the tense in italics. An example has been done for you.*

Ex. "See you in the morning, Recreation Director!" he **call**, dismounting by his door as Asher continued on.

a) subject: ___he___ b) **bold** verb in *past* tense: ___called___

c) Sentence in *present* tense: "See you in the morning, Recreation Director!" he *calls*, dismounting by his door as Asher *continues* on.

1. He **imagine** Benjamin, the scientific male in his group, beginning to read pages of rules and instructions with relish.

   a) subject: ________________ b) **bold** verb in *future* tense: ____________

   c) Sentence in *past* tense: ____

   ____

2. It **be** an integral part of the learning of precise speech.

   a) subject: ________________ b) **bold** verb in *past* tense: ____________

   c) Sentence in *present* tense: ____

   ____

3. Then she **seem** to notice his discomfort and to realize its origin.

   a) subject: ________________ b) **bold** verb in *present* tense: ____________

   c) Sentence in *future* tense: ____

   ____

Name ____ Period ____________

4. The fabrics on the upholstered chairs and sofa **was** slightly thicker and more luxurious; the table legs were not straight like those at home, but slender and curved, with a small carved decoration at the foot.

   a) subject: ________________ b) **bold** verb in *present* tense: ___________

   c) Sentence in *future* tense: ____

   ____

5. "But that does not mean I am perfect, and when I tried to train a successor, I **will fail**."

   a) subject: ________________ b) **bold** verb in *past* tense: ______________

   c) Sentence in *present* tense: ____

   ____

6. Jonas **do** so, a little apprehensively.

   a) subject: ________________ b) **bold** verb in *future* tense: ____________

   c) Sentence in *present* tense: ____

   ____

7. In each dwelling tonight they **are studying** the instructions for the beginning of their training.

   a) subject: ________________ b) **bold** verb in *future* tense: ____________

   c) Sentence in *past* tense: ____

   ____

8. A name designated Not-to-Be-Spoken **indicated** the highest degree of disgrace.

   a) subject: ________________ b) **bold** verb in *present* tense: ___________

   c) Sentence in *future* tense: ____

   ____

9. He **will wonder** briefly, though, how to deal with it at the morning meal.

   a) subject: ________________ b) **bold** verb in *past* tense: ______________

   c) Sentence in *present* tense: ____

   ____

10. He certainly **does**n't **want** to be late for his first day of training, either.

    a) subject: ________________ b) **bold** verb in *future* tense: ____________

    c) Sentence in *past* tense: ____

    ____

Name ____ Period ____________

Chapters Eleven—Twelve
Note-Taking and Summarizing: Chapter 11

Setting	
Characters	
Summary of the Chapter	
Prediction of Coming Events	

Name ____ Period ____________

Note-Taking and Summarizing: Chapter 12

Setting	
Characters	
Summary of the Chapter	
Prediction of Coming Events	

Name ______________________________________ Period ___________

Chapters Eleven—Twelve Comprehension Check

Directions: *To help you understand all aspects of the novel, answer the following questions for Chapters 11-12. Write your answers on a separate piece of paper using complete sentences.*

Chapter Eleven

1. Describe the memory The Giver transmits to Jonas.
2. Discuss how Jonas feels about the memory he receives.
3. Compare a new experience that you enjoyed to Jonas's first experience of snow.
4. Explain the two ways in which Jonas can see.
5. Based on The Giver's comments, measure the age of the community.
6. Name aspects of nature that were eliminated when the community went to Sameness.
7. Distinguish between honor and power as they refer to The Giver's position in the community.
8. Examine how the process of receiving a memory works.
9. Infer why the gentleman's title changed to The Giver.

Chapter Twelve

1. Describe how Gabriel sleeps.
2. Discuss the dream that Jonas has. How does Jonas feel about the dream when he wakes up?
3. Relate how Jonas's position makes him feel different from his classmates.
4. Infer why the Old are punished for disobedience and what the punishment says about the community's culture.
5. List the three examples of "seeing beyond" that Jonas experiences.
6. Generalize what seeing beyond means.
7. Contrast The Giver's memories with the memories of the other citizens in the community.
8. What does the world look like to the citizens of this community?
9. List items over which the community gained control and items they let go. Was the trade-off worth it? Would you want to give up these things? Why or why not? Give reasons to support your answer.

Name ____ Period ____________

Chapters Eleven— Twelve
Standards Focus: Elements of Style

An author's **style** is what differentiates his/her writing from the work of other authors. Sentence structure, descriptive language, tone, word choice, rhythm, repetition, figurative language, and vocabulary all contribute to an author's distinctive style. An author's style can affect how the reader interacts with and understands the text.

Lois Lowry uses a variety of techniques to create a style that makes *The Giver* a modern-day classic. She utilizes factual tone, symbolism, sensory images, point of view, precise word choice, repetition, sentence fragments, and unusual proper nouns to formulate the novel's style.

Directions: *Identify the elements of style that have been underlined in the following passages. Elements may be used more than once. Once you have identified the elements of style that have been used in each excerpt, explain the effect that these stylistic techniques have on the reader. An example has been done for you.*

factual tone	symbolism	sensory images
first person point of view	repetition	sentence fragments
unusual proper nouns	precise word choice	descriptive vocabulary

Ex. *It was very startling (A); but he was not at all frightened, now. He was filled with energy, and he breathed again, feeling the sharp intake of frigid air (B). Now, too, he could feel cold air swirling around his entire body (C). He felt it blow against his hands where they lay at his sides, and over his back.*

Elements of style: A. precise word choice; B. sensory image, descriptive vocabulary; C. sensory image

Effect: The author begins the description with the strong word "startling" and not just the word "scary." The description includes sensory images which allow the reader to feel the frigid air that Jonas experiences, helping to create an image in the reader's mind.

1. Finally the obstruction of the piled snow was too much for the thin runners of the sled, and he came to a stop. He sat there for a moment, panting, holding the rope (A) in his cold hands. Tentatively (B) he opened his eyes – not his snow-hill-sled eyes (C), for they had been open throughout the strange ride. He opened his ordinary eyes, and saw that he was still on the bed, that he had not moved at all.

   Elements of style: A. ________________________ B. ________________________

   C. ________________________

Name ____ Period ____________

Effect: ____

____

____

____

2. "And hills, too," he added. "They made conveyance of goods unwieldy. (A) Trucks; buses. Slowed them down. So—" (B) He waved his hand, as if a gesture had caused hills to disappear. "Sameness," he concluded.

Elements of style: A. ______________________ B.______________________

Effect: ____

____

____

____

3. He was left, upon awakening, with the feeling that he wanted, even somehow needed, to reach the something that waited in the distance. The feeling that it was good. (A) That it was welcoming. That it was significant. (B)

Elements of style: A. ______________________ B.______________________

Effect: ____

____

____

____

4. "Oh, there's lots to learn," Fiona replied. "There's administrative work, and the dietary rules, and punishment for disobedience (A) – did you know that they use a discipline wand on the Old (B), the same as for small children? And there's occupational therapy, and recreational activities, and medications, and—"

Elements of style: A. ______________________ B. ______________________

Effect: ____

____

____

____

Name ____ Period ____________

Chapters Eleven— Twelve
Assessment Preparation: Synonyms and Antonyms

Directions: *Using a thesaurus and/or a dictionary, fill in one synonym and one antonym for each of the vocabulary words. Then write a sentence using the vocabulary word, showing that you understand the word's meaning and how it should be used in a sentence.*

1. **torrent** synonym: __________________ antonym: __________________

sentence: ____

____

2. **glee** synonym: __________________ antonym: __________________

sentence: ____

____

3. **obsolete** synonym: __________________ antonym: __________________

sentence: ____

____

4. **wincing** synonym: __________________ antonym: __________________

sentence: ____

____

5. **admonition** synonym: __________________ antonym: __________________

sentence: ____

____

6. **dumbfounded** synonym: __________________ antonym: __________________

sentence: ____

____

7. **wryly** synonym: __________________ antonym: __________________

sentence: ____

____

Name ____ Period ____________

Chapters Thirteen—Fourteen

Note-Taking and Summarizing: Chapter 13

Setting	
Characters	
Summary of the Chapter	
Prediction of Coming Events	

Name ____ Period ____________

Note-Taking and Summarizing: Chapter 14

Setting	
Characters	
Summary of the Chapter	
Prediction of Coming Events	

Name ____ Period ____________

Chapters Thirteen—Fourteen Comprehension Check

Directions: *To help you understand all aspects of the novel, answer the following questions for Chapters 13-14. Write your answers on a separate piece of paper using complete sentences.*

Chapter Thirteen

1. What is happening to the colors that Jonas sees?
2. Discuss why Jonas wants to select the color of his tunic.
3. Discuss experiences in which you are or have been protected from making poor choices.
4. In your opinion, would it be worse to suffer the consequences of making poor choices or not to be able to make choices at all?
5. What do you think would have happened if Jonas had successfully transmitted memories to Asher and Lily?
6. Through memories, Jonas learns about grief. Explain how the community's structures usually prevent the citizens from experiencing grief. Why is this a good or a bad thing?
7. Summarize why it would be challenging for the Receiver to be part of a family unit.
8. Relate the differences in how Jonas, the Elders, and The Giver view "life."
9. Infer what would happen in the community if all the citizens had access to the memories.

Chapter Fourteen

1. Assess how Jonas's new memory of sledding differs from his previous memories of sledding. What does this memory symbolize?
2. Tell why Jonas does not take any medicine for the pain from his sledding memory.
3. How do the citizens' reasons for wanting to increase the birth rate relate to the overall goal of the community?
4. Calculate how the past famine and war may have contributed to the community's current structure.
5. Explain how the roles of Giver and Receiver ensure order in the community.
6. Explain the plan by which Jonas and The Giver attempt to change the structure of the community.
7. Create an argument to try to convince the Elders that memories should be available to everyone in the community.
8. List areas in which Gabriel has and has not met the Nurturers' standards.
9. Describe Jonas's beliefs about Elsewhere.
10. Relate how the two times in which Jonas transmits a memory to Gabriel differ.
11. Jonas broke a rule by transmitting a memory to Gabriel. Should Jonas turn himself in for this infraction? Why or why not?

Name ______________________________ Period __________

Chapters Thirteen—Fourteen
Standards Focus: Conflict

Conflict results from two opposing forces in a story. Four common types of conflict are:

Man vs. himself—a character experiences conflict between forces within him/herself
Man vs. man—a character experiences a conflict with another person
Man vs. nature—a character struggles to overcome forces of nature
Man vs. society—a character struggles with elements of his/her society

Directions: *Read each passage from Chapters 13-14. Identify which type of conflict it exemplifies and explain it.*

Ex. "Well . . ." Jonas had to stop and think it through. "If everything's the same, then there aren't any choices! I want to wake up in the morning and *decide* things! A blue tunic, or a red one?"

He looked down at himself, at the colorless fabric of his clothing. "But it's all the same, always." (pg. 97)

Type of conflict: man vs. society

Explanation: Jonas is frustrated with the restrictions and lack of choices placed on his life by the community's structure.

1. But when the conversation turned to other things, Jonas was left, still, with a feeling of frustration that he didn't understand.

He found that he was often angry, now: irrationally angry at his groupmates, that they were satisfied with their lives which had none of the vibrance his own was taking on. And he was angry at himself, that he could not change that for them. (pg. 99)

Type of conflict: ______________________________

Explanation: ______________________________

____

2. Jonas went and sat beside them while his father untied Lily's hair ribbons and combed her hair. He placed one hand on each of their shoulders. With all of his being he tried to give each of them a piece of the memory . . .

But his father had continued to comb Lily's long hair, and Lily, impatient, had finally wiggled under her brother's touch. "Jonas," she said, "you're *hurting* me with your hand." (pg. 101)

Type of conflict: ______________________________

Explanation: ______________________________

____

3. "When you become the official Receiver, when we're finished here, you'll be given a whole new set of rules. Those are the rules that I obey. And it won't surprise you that I

Name ____ Period ____________

am forbidden to talk about my work to anyone except the new Receiver. That's you, of course." (pg. 103)

Type of conflict: ____

Explanation: ____

____

4. By himself, he (Jonas) tested his own developing memory. He watched the landscape for glimpses of the green that he knew was embedded in the shrubbery; when it came flickering into his consciousness, he focused upon it, keeping it there, darkening it, holding it in his vision as long as possible until his head hurt and he let it fade away. (pg. 106)

Type of conflict: ____

Explanation: ____

____

5. The sled moved forward, and Jonas grinned with delight, looking forward to the breathtaking slide down through the invigorating air.

But the runners, this time, couldn't slice through the frozen expanse as they had on the other, snow-cushioned hill. They skittered sideways and the sled gathered speed. Jonas pulled at the rope, trying to steer, but the steepness and speed took control from his hands and he was no longer enjoying the feeling of freedom but instead, terrified, was at the mercy of the wild acceleration downward over the ice. (pg. 108)

Type of conflict: ____

Explanation: ____

____

6. "I knew that there had been times in the past—terrible times—when people had destroyed others in haste, in fear, and had brought about their own destruction." (pg. 112)

Type of conflict: ____

Explanation: ____

____

7. He wondered, though, if he should confess to The Giver that he had given a memory away. He was not yet qualified to be a Giver himself; nor had Gabriel been selected to be a Receiver.

That he had this power frightened him. He decided not to tell. (pg. 117)

Type of conflict: ____

Explanation: ____

____

Name ____ Period ____________

Chapters Thirteen— Fourteen
Assessment Preparation: Vocabulary Extension

Directions: *(1) Using the vocabulary words from the list below, select the word that best completes the sentence. Each word will be used only once. (2) Then write an original sentence using each vocabulary word on a separate piece of paper and staple it to this worksheet when you are finished.*

irrationally	sinuous	assimilated	embedded
agony	assuage	ominous	placidly

1. The wind had a/an _________________________ sound before the tornado struck.

2. The __________________ snake curled up in the tree.

3. After Adam broke his leg, he was in ___________________ until the doctor set it.

4. The infant played __________________ in her crib as she listened to lullabies.

5. Patrick worried _______________________ that his parents would lose him in the crowd at the football game.

6. The archaeologist delicately removed the _____________________ fossils from the rock.

7. Even though it was an accident, nothing could _____________________ Sarah's guilt for causing the collision.

8. The welcoming community _______________________ many immigrants into it over the years.

Name ____ Period ____________

Chapters Fifteen—Seventeen

Note-Taking and Summarizing: Chapters 15-16

Setting	
Characters	
Summary of the Chapter	
Prediction of Coming Events	

Name ____ Period ____________

Note-Taking and Summarizing: Chapter 17

Setting	
Characters	
Summary of the Chapter	
Prediction of Coming Events	

Name ____ Period ____________

Chapters Fifteen—Seventeen
Comprehension Check

Directions: *To help you understand all aspects of the novel, answer the following questions for Chapters 15-17. Write your answers on a separate piece of paper using complete sentences.*

Chapters Fifteen—Sixteen

1. Contrast how you experience history with how the Receiver experiences it.
2. The community was partly created to avoid war in the future. Decide whether Jonas would prefer to live in the community or in a society with war. Give reasons to support your answer.
3. Describe how Jonas's life differs from the lives of his classmates.
4. Create a chart which lists positive and negative qualities of the outside world that Jonas has experienced through the memories.
5. Show how extended families in the community differ from extended families in our society.
6. Jonas tells The Giver, "I just didn't realize there was any other way, until I received that memory." Predict how the memory of a family at Christmas will affect Jonas's feelings about the community. Give reasons to support your answer.
7. Jonas is amazed by the feeling of love he observes among the family members in the memory. Analyze how a family in our society would function without love between its members.
8. Who does Jonas wish could be his grandparent? Is this possible?
9. Any form of risk is avoided in the community. Examine the types of risk we experience in our daily lives.
10. Explain how being proud of someone is not the same thing as loving them. Do you think Jonas's parents understand the concept of love? Why or why not?
11. What does Jonas admit to Gabriel? How does Jonas convey love to Gabriel?

Chapter Seventeen

1. What effect does discontinuing the pills have on Jonas?
2. Discuss why Jonas reacts so strongly to the game played by his groupmates.
3. Explain the statement, "he [Jonas] knew that such times had been taken from him now."
4. Explain what Father must do after the identical twins are born.

Name ____ Period ____________

Chapters Fifteen—Seventeen
Standards Focus: Theme

Themes are the central ideas in a work of literature. The themes must often be inferred by carefully examining the characters' words and actions, as well as the plot, setting, and mood of the novel. Themes can be concrete objects such as family and friends, ideas like love and individuality, and experiences such as survival and human connection.

Directions: *Read and answer the questions about the following excerpts from the novel. After examining each pair of quotes, use them to infer a theme from the novel.*

First Pair:
Jonas trudged to the bench beside the Storehouse and sat down, overwhelmed with feelings of loss. His childhood, his friendships, his carefree sense of security—all of these things seemed to be slipping away. (pg. 135)

1. What does Jonas miss about his childhood? ______________________________

____

"Warmth," Jonas replied, and happiness. And—let me think. Family. That it was a celebration of some sort, a holiday. And something else—I can't quite get the word for it."

. . . Jonas hesitated. "I certainly liked the memory, though. I can see why it's your favorite. I couldn't quite get the word for the whole feeling for it, the feeling that was so strong in the room."

"Love," The Giver told him.

Jonas repeated it. "Love." It was a word and concept new to him. (pg. 123, 125)

2. How does Jonas "see" love in the memory? ______________________________

____

____

3. How do these passages illustrate Jonas's desire for human connection? ________

____

____

What theme does this first pair of quotes reveal? ______________________________

____

Second Pair:
"You Elevens have spent all your years till now learning to fit in, to standardize your behavior, to curb any impulse that might set you apart from the group." (pgs. 51-52)

Name ____ Period _____________

4. How does standardizing one's appearance and behavior help the Elevens fit into their group? ____
____
____

He had seen a birthday party, with one child singled out and celebrated on his day, so that now he understood the joy of being an individual, special and unique and proud. (pg. 121)

5. Why is Jonas so intrigued by the birthday party? _________________________
____

6. How does a person in Jonas's community balance being an individual with being a contributing member of society? _________________________________
____
____
____

7. How is this different from being an individual in our society? _____________
____
____

What theme does this second pair of quotes reveal? __________________________
____

Third Pair:
With his new, heightened feelings, he was overwhelmed by sadness at the way the others had laughed and shouted, playing at war. But he knew that they could not understand why, without the memories. (pg. 135)

8. How are the memories influencing Jonas's present life? ___________________
____
____

"It seems to work pretty well that way, doesn't it? The way we do it in our community?" Jonas asked. "I just didn't realize there was any other way, until I received that memory." (pg. 125)

9. What do the memories show Jonas about a different way of life? _____________
____

Name ____ Period ____________

____

____

10. What does the community lose by not having memories? What does it gain? ____

____

____

What theme does this third pair of quotes reveal? ____________________________

____

Fourth Pair:

Jonas nodded. "I liked the feeling of love," he confessed. He glanced nervously at the speaker on the wall, reassuring himself that no one was listening. "I wish we still had that," he whispered. "Of course," he added quickly, "I do understand that it wouldn't work very well. And that it's much better to be organized the way we are now. I can see that it was a dangerous *way to live."* (pg. 126)

11. Why does Jonas think it was "dangerous" way to live? ____________________

____

____

"Things could change, Gabe," Jonas went on. "Things could be different. I don't know how, but there must be some way for things to be different. There could be colors.

"And grandparents," he added, staring through the dimness toward the ceiling of his sleepingroom. "And everybody would have the memories." (pg. 128)

12. What would Jonas like to change about the community? ____________________

____

____

13. How could Jonas change his society? Do you think he would be more successful working for change from within or outside of the community? ____________

____

____

____

What theme does this fourth pair of quotes reveal? ___________________________

____

Name ____ Period ____________

Chapters Fifteen—Seventeen
Assessment Preparation: Punctuation

Punctuation assists the reader when interpreting a text. Commas tell the reader when to pause; periods inform the reader when the writer completes a thought; quotation marks notify the reader when a character is speaking; question marks cue an interrogative sentence.

Directions: *Rewrite the following sentences with correct punctuation on the lines provided.*

1. Put your hands on me he directed aware that in such anguish The Giver might need reminding ____
____
____

2. In one ecstatic memory he had ridden a gleaming brown horse across a field that smelled of damp grass and had dismounted beside a small stream from which both he and the horse drank cold clear water ________________________________
____
____
____
____

3. It seems to work pretty well that way doesn't it The way we do it in our community Jonas asked ____
____
____

4. Thinking as he always did about precision of language Jonas realized that it was a new depth of feelings that he was experiencing ________________________
____
____

Name ______________________________________ Period ____________

5. Now he had in the memories experienced injustice and cruelty and he had reacted with rage that welled up so passionately inside him that the thought of discussing it calmly at the evening meal was unthinkable ______________________________
____
____
____
____

6. I'm the one who's training for Assistant Recreation Director Asher pointed out angrily Games aren't your area of expertness ____________________________________
____
____

7. Jonas trudged to the bench beside the Storehouse and sat down overwhelmed with feelings of loss ____
____
____

8. Do you actually take it Elsewhere Father Jonas asked ____________________
____

9. What is your favorite Jonas asked The Giver ___________________________
____

10. The small child went and sat on the lap of the old woman and she rocked him and rubbed her cheek against his ____
____
____

Name ______________________________________ Period ____________

Chapters Eighteen—Twenty

Note-Taking and Summarizing: Chapters 18-19

Setting	
Characters	
Summary of the Chapter	
Prediction of Coming Events	

Name ____ Period ____________

Note-Taking and Summarizing: Chapter 20

Setting	
Characters	
Summary of the Chapter	
Prediction of Coming Events	

Name ____ Period ____________

Chapters Eighteen—Twenty Comprehension Check

Directions: *To help you understand all aspects of the novel, answer the following questions for Chapters 18-20. Write your answers on a separate piece of paper using complete sentences.*

Chapter Eighteen

1. What rule was added to the Receiver's job description ten years ago?
2. Compare and contrast Rosemary and Jonas.
3. Examine the irony of Rosemary being stunned by the memory of a child being taken from its parents.
4. Explain why Rosemary applied for release.
5. Generalize what would happen to the memories if Jonas disappeared.

Chapter Nineteen

1. Infer why identical twins are not allowed in the community.
2. Why do you think The Giver encourages Jonas to watch the video of the twin's release? Should The Giver have done this? Why or why not?
3. What does Jonas's father do to the infant?
4. Show how an actual release differs from Jonas's expectations of one.
5. Explain how seeing the release changed Jonas's opinion of his father.
6. Assess if Rosemary truly understood release before she asked for one. How did Rosemary choose to deal with the memories?

Chapter Twenty

1. Does Jonas feel more attached to his family unit or to The Giver? Give reasons to support your answer.
2. Explain how the infant is a metaphor for Jonas.
3. Relate how the memories empower as well as destroy Jonas.
4. Discuss how The Giver wants to change the community from within.
5. How did The Giver first experience life beyond the community?
6. Infer why Jonas and The Giver think a society exists outside the community.
7. Summarize Jonas's escape plan.
8. Conclude why The Giver believes Rosemary is his daughter. How does he think he can be with her?
9. Decide what the author foreshadows at the end of this chapter. What clues lead you to this conclusion?

Name ____ Period ____________

Chapters Eighteen—Twenty
Standards Focus: Character Development

An author reveals information about a novel's **characters** in a variety of ways. A character may provide information about him or herself by sharing his/her thoughts, words, and actions with the reader. Likewise, a narrator or other characters can also provide the reader with insight about a particular person.

Directions: *Using the clues, locate specific quotes or descriptions about Jonas to show examples of his behavior or personality throughout the novel. Use these excerpts to write a paragraph about Jonas on the next page.*

1. How Jonas feels about the upcoming Ceremony (Chapter 1): ________________
____
____
2. What Jonas initially believes release is like (Chapter 4): ____________________
____
____
3. How Jonas feels about the Elders' decisions (Chapter 6): ___________________
____
____
4. When Jonas experiences seeing beyond (Chapter 8): _______________________
____
____
5. When Jonas learns of a world beyond the community (Chapter 10): ___________
____
____
6. How Jonas feels about the world outside the community (Chapter 12): ________
____
____
7. How Jonas feels about all the citizens having memories (Chapter 14): _________
____
____
8. When Jonas learns about love and real families (Chapter 16): ______________
____
____

Name ____ Period ____________

9. When Jonas disagrees with the community's practices (Chapter 20): __________
____
____

10. On the lines below, write 1-2 paragraphs detailing how Jonas and his opinion of the community change from the beginning of the novel through Chapter 20. Use statements and quotes from the novel to support your argument.

____
____
____
____
____
____
____
____
____
____
____
____
____
____
____
____
____
____
____
____
____
____
____
____

Name ____ Period ____________

Chapters Eighteen—Twenty
Assessment Preparation: Precise Word Choice

Authors carefully select the words they use when writing. Using a specific word can subtly change the mood, strength, and meaning of a text.

Directions: *Below are excerpts from the novel that include precise language. Rewrite each sentence substituting a similar, but less specific, word for the word in bold print. Then explain why the bold-print word more effectively conveys the author's meaning. An example has been completed for you. Use your definitions list or a dictionary for help.*

Ex. "Me," Jonas said in a **dejected** voice. He was not looking forward to the end of the training, when he would become the new Receiver.

a. Rewrite Sentence: "Me," Jonas said in a depressed voice. He was not looking forward to the end of the training, when he would become the new Receiver.

b. Explanation: Dejected conveys the depth of Jonas's sadness, and that he does not want to be the new Receiver. Depressed just tells the reader that Jonas is sad.

1. The Giver hesitated painfully, as if saying the name aloud might be **excruciating**. "Her name was Rosemary," he told Jonas, finally.

   a. Rewrite Sentence: ____
   ____

   b. Explanation: ____
   ____

2. "I [Giver] couldn't bring myself to **inflict** physical pain on her [Rosemary]."

   a. Rewrite Sentence: ____
   ____

   b. Explanation: ____
   ____

3. "I wish I could watch," he [Jonas] added, as an **afterthought**.

   a. Rewrite Sentence: ____
   ____

   b. Explanation: ____
   ____

Name ______________________________ Period __________

4. "I [Giver] do know that I sat here numb with horror. **Wretched** with helplessness."

   a. Rewrite Sentence: ______________________________

   ____

   b. Explanation: ______________________________

   ____

5. "I [Giver] am **empowered** to lie. But I have never lied to you [Jonas]."

   a. Rewrite Sentence: ______________________________

   ____

   b. Explanation: ______________________________

   ____

6. "I [Giver] think that they [citizens] can, and that they will **acquire** some wisdom."

   a. Rewrite Sentence: ______________________________

   ____

   b. Explanation: ______________________________

   ____

7. Confronted by a situation which they [citizens] had never faced before, and having no memories from which to find either **solace** or wisdom, they would not know what to do and would seek his [Giver's] advice.

   a. Rewrite Sentence: ______________________________

   ____

   b. Explanation: ______________________________

   ____

Name ____ Period ____________

Chapters Twenty-One—Twenty-Three

Note-Taking and Summarizing: Chapter 21

Setting	
Characters	
Summary of the Chapter	
Prediction of Coming Events	

Name ______________________________________ Period ____________

Note-Taking and Summarizing: Chapters 22-23

Setting	
Characters	
Summary of the Chapter	
Prediction of Coming Events	

Name ____ Period ____________

Chapters Twenty-One—Twenty-Three
Comprehension Check

Directions: *To help you understand all aspects of the novel, answer the following questions for Chapters 21-23. Write your answers on a separate piece of paper using complete sentences.*

Chapter Twenty-One

1. What forces Jonas to flee the community sooner than he had planned?
2. Discuss how Jonas staying overnight with The Giver leads to the decision to release Gabriel.
3. Show how the author lets the reader believe that Gabriel has been released.
4. Infer why citizens may not leave their dwellings at night or remove extra food from the community.
5. Create a different escape plan for Jonas and Gabriel.
6. Explain how Jonas nurtures Gabriel more than the Nurturers did. Explain the irony in the newchildren's caretakers being called Nurturers.
7. Describe how the author uses planes to bookend the novel. What do you believe is her purpose?
8. How well do you think The Giver's plan to return memories to the community works?
9. Relate how the author introduces elements of science fiction into this chapter.
10. Estimate how far Jonas and Gabriel have traveled and if they are still in the communities.

Chapter Twenty-Two

1. Analyze how the natural world changes as Jonas and Gabriel travel farther from their community.
2. Discriminate between Jonas's and Father's methods of nurturing Gabriel.
3. Tell how Jonas's survival instincts while he is fleeing the community differ from when he lived in the community.
4. Differentiate how Jonas feels about his survival compared to Gabriel's.

Chapter Twenty-Three

1. Examine what Jonas experiences: Is the snow just a figment of his imagination? Is the snow real? Is Jonas freezing and/or starving to death?
2. Contrast Gabriel when he is fleeing the community to how he was when he lived in the community.
3. Imagine and describe what the boundary between the communities and the outside world looks like.
4. Assess if Jonas is dreaming, dying, or really escaping the community. Think about whether a sled would be waiting if the scene is real.
5. What clues lead the reader to think that Jonas is reaching the Elsewhere that he thought existed?
6. Lois Lowry intended the ending of the novel to be ambiguous. Do you like the ending? Why or why not? Discuss other possibilities for the conclusion of the novel.

Name ____ Period ____________

Chapters Twenty-One—Twenty-Three
Standards Focus: Elements of Plot

Plot is the related series of events that create the action in a novel. There are several parts of a plot:

- **Exposition**- the beginning of the novel that gives background information on the setting and characters
- **Rising action**- the development of complications and problems within the novel
- **Climax**- the turning point of the novel when the protagonist makes an important decision that often changes the direction of the story
- **Falling action**- the action that occurs after the climax when the story begins to wrap up
- **Resolution**- the conclusion of the novel when the loose ends are tied up

***Directions**: Complete the chart below, filling in each box with a short description of the action that corresponds with each box.*

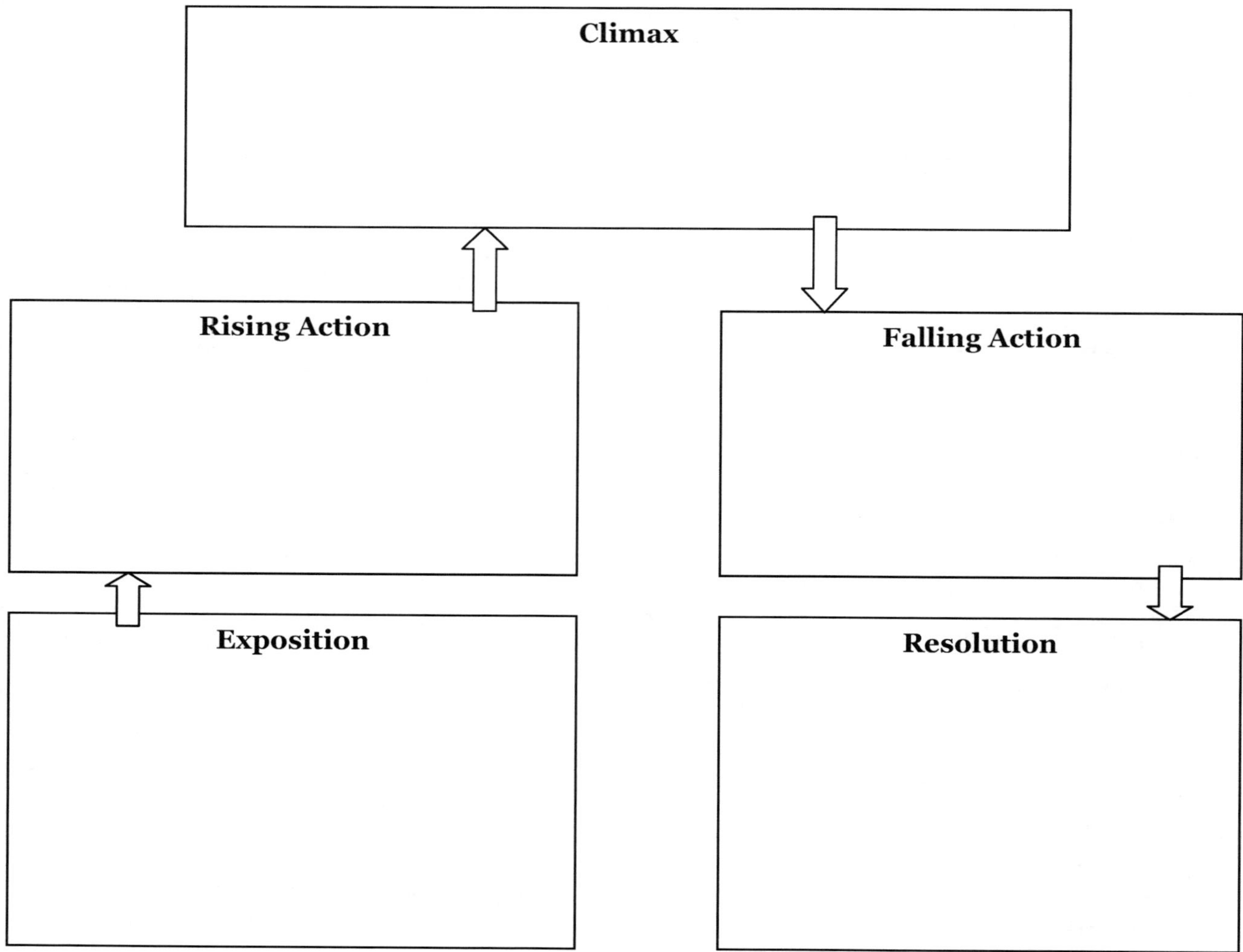

Name ____ Period ____________

Chapters Twenty-One—Twenty-Three
Assessment Preparation: Sentence Structure

A **simple sentence** consists of a *subject* that tells who or what the sentence is about and a *predicate* that tells something about the subject. *Ex. Mary ate lunch.*

A **simple sentence with a compound subject** contains two or more connected subjects that have the same verb. *Ex. Mary and Umberto ate lunch.*

A **simple sentence with a compound verb** consists of one subject with two verbs. *Ex. Mary ate lunch and relaxed.*

A **compound sentence** contains two or more simple sentences connected by a conjunction such as *and, but, or, nor, for*, or *yet*. *Ex. Mary ate lunch* ***and*** *Umberto went shopping.*

Directions*: Underline the subject(s) of each sentence one time and circle the verb(s). Then, label each sentence as a simple sentence, a simple sentence with a compound subject, a simple sentence with a compound verb, or a compound sentence.*

1. He could see the dark, churning water far below. (pg. 163)

   Type of sentence: ____

2. Jonas put down his fork and stared at his father. (pg. 165)

   Type of sentence: ____

3. They were stronger, and he stopped now less often to rest. (pg. 168)

   Type of sentence: ____

4. The Instructor and class waited patiently for his explanation. (pg. 3)

   Type of sentence: ____

5. Jonas knelt by a stream and tried without success to catch a fish with his hands. (pg. 173)

   Type of sentence: ____

6. The memory was agonizingly brief. (pg. 177)

   Type of sentence: ____

7. They had to leave very early, and they had their midday meal on the bus. (pg. 6)

   Type of sentence: ____

Name ____ Period ____________

The Giver
Quiz: Chapters 1-2

Directions: *CIRCLE the letter of the best answer for each of the following questions. WRITE the letter of the best choice on the lines provided at the bottom of the page.*

1. What are the citizens told to do when the Pilot accidentally flies over the community?
   a. watch the plane b. go inside
   c. shoot at the plane d. ignore the plane

2. What must Asher do when he is late to class?
   a. apologize to the entire class b. sneak into class
   c. skip school that day d. stay after school for detention

3. Why may the male infant that Father discusses at dinner be released?
   a. He is not walking. b. He cannot sit up.
   c. He cannot feed himself. d. He does not sleep soundly at night.

4. Which is *not* a reason that someone may be released?
   a. punishment b. reward
   c. elderly d. infant not thriving

5. What must families do at dinner each evening?
   a. tell the best and worst parts of their days b. make plans for the next day
   c. tell their feelings d. bless the food

6. What happens each December?
   a. ceremony when each child gets older b. Christmas celebration
   c. Winter begins d. everyone goes on vacation

7. Where do newchildren live for their first year?
   a. with their mothers b. with foster families
   c. with their fathers d. at the Nurturing Center

8. How does Father attempt to enhance Gabriel's nurturing?
   a. feeds him an extra bottle b. calls him by the name he will be given
   c. plays with him more d. snuggles with him more

9. Which statement is *false* regarding the milestones of becoming a Twelve?
   a. children stop going to school b. age is no longer important
   c. Assignments are given d. volunteer hours end

10. Who is the most important Elder in the community?
    a. Nurturer b. Birthmother
    c. Receiver d. Chief Elder

1. ______ 2. ______ 3. ______ 4. ______ 5. ______

6. ______ 7. ______ 8. ______ 9. ______ 10. ______

Name ______________________________ Period __________

The Giver
Quiz: Chapters 3-4

Directions: *Answer the following questions using complete sentences. Give as many details as possible to support your response.*

1. How are Birthmothers regarded in the community?

 ____
 ____
 ____
 ____

2. How are individual differences and appearances treated in the community?

 ____
 ____
 ____

3. Why does Jonas take the apple home?

 ____
 ____
 ____

4. How do the Ceremony of Twelve and a Ceremony of Release treat people as individuals?

 ____
 ____
 ____
 ____

5. What does the author mean by "Assignment"?

 ____
 ____
 ____

6. What things are provided to citizens in the community?

 ____
 ____
 ____
 ____

Name ____ Period ____________

The Giver
Vocabulary Quiz: Chapters 1-4

Directions: *Match the vocabulary words for numbers 1-8 with the correct definition from letters a-h. Then match the vocabulary words in numbers 9-16 with the correct definition from letters i-p. Write the letter of the correct definition or synonym on the line provided.*

1. ______ ironic
2. ______ palpable
3. ______ wheedle
4. ______ disposition
5. ______ transgression
6. ______ awed
7. ______ technically
8. ______ aptitude

a. to influence someone through flattery or trickery
b. strictly; based on legal interpretation
c. the opposite of intended or expected meaning
d. brought up feelings of amazement or fear
e. natural ability
f. noticeable; intense; obvious
g. breaking a law or rule
h. personality; attitude

- -

9. _______ chastise
10. ______ petulantly
11. ______ remorse
12. ______ conviction
13. ______ hasten
14. ______ tabulated
15. ______ nuisance
16. ______ chortled

i. belief
j. annoying or unpleasant
k. in a touchy, sullen, or grumpy manner
l. calculated
m. laughed; giggled
n. to correct or punish
o. move or act quickly
p. a strong feeling of guilt

Name ____ Period ___________

The Giver
Quiz: Chapters 5-6

Directions: *For each of the following statements, write "true" if the statement is true, and "false" if the statement is false. For each of the false statements, use the lines below the statement to rewrite the sentence, making the statement true.*

1. ____________At breakfast each morning, the family unit tells their feelings. _____

____

2. ____________When citizens are elderly, they live at the House of the Old. ______

____

3. ____________Citizens take a pill each day to eliminate Stirrings. ___________

____

4. ____________Christmas is the major celebration in the community. __________

____

5. ____________Gabriel fell in the river and drowned. ____________________

____

6. ____________The Elders decide each citizen's Assignment. ______________

____

7. ____________At the age of one, newchildren are placed with a family, and families select names for their children. ________________________________

____

8. ____________Thirteens are given an Assignment. ____________________

____

9. ____________Eights begin serving volunteer hours. ___________________

____

Name ____ Period ____________

The Giver
Quiz: Chapters 7-8

Directions: *CIRCLE the letter of the best answer for each of the following questions. WRITE the letter of the best choice on the lines provided at the bottom of the page.*

1. Before being named, newchildren are
   a. identified by describing their appearance
   b. identified by a number corresponding to the order in which they were born
   c. identified by their parents' names
   d. identified by a letter corresponding to the order in which they were born

2. The Chief Elder is
   a. elected every ten years
   b. appointed by a committee
   c. elected every five years
   d. expected to serve for his/her lifetime

3. Asher's Assignment is
   a. Instructor of Eights
   b. Assistant Director of the Landscape Crew
   c. Assistant Director of Recreation
   d. Pilot

4. To select a Receiver-in-Training
   a. the community votes for an individual
   b. the previous Receiver selects him/her by himself
   c. a person volunteers for the Assignment
   d. the Elders meticulously observe the students

5. Which of the following is not a rule for the Receiver-in-Training?
   a. the person is to be alone
   b. the person may refuse the Assignment
   c. the person must be apart from the community
   d. the position cannot be modified

6. Which five qualities must the Receiver possess?
   a. Intelligence, Integrity, Courage, Wisdom, and the Capacity to See Beyond
   b. Intelligence, Integrity, Imagination, Wisdom, and the Capacity to See Beyond
   c. Curiosity, Integrity, Courage, Wisdom, and the Capacity to See Beyond
   d. Intelligence, Integrity, Courage, Wisdom, and Patience

1. _______ 2. _______ 3. _______ 4. _______ 5. _______ 6. _______

Name ______________________________________ Period ____________

The Giver
Vocabulary Quiz: Chapters 5-8

Directions: *Write the vocabulary word that best matches each definition, choosing from the word bank below. Be careful to spell the word correctly as you write. Not all words will be used.*

aptitude	avert	benign	disquieting
emblem	exuberant	indolence	infringed
meticulously	nuisance	palpable	prestige
profound	relinquish	reprieve	retroactive
spontaneously	throng	unanimous	

1. delay of punishment: ______________________________
2. to turn away: ______________________________
3. very carefully; scrupulously: ______________________________
4. high standing in others' opinions: ______________________________
5. causing a feeling of anxiety; disturbing: ______________________________
6. occurring naturally; without being planned: ______________________________
7. full of enthusiasm; lively: ______________________________
8. laziness; lack of interest: ______________________________
9. something that visually symbolizes an object, idea, group, or quality; a symbol:

   ____
10. deep, strong, or intense: ______________________________
11. intruded upon land, rights, or privileges that belong to someone else:

    ____
12. mild; harmless: ______________________________
13. all members of a group in complete agreement: ______________________________
14. to give up; surrender: ______________________________
15. relating or applying to things that have happened in the past: ______________________________

Name ______________________________ Period ____________

The Giver
Quiz: Chapters 9-10

Directions: *Answer the following questions using complete sentences. Give details to support your response.*

1. List the rules Jonas receives for his training as Receiver of Memory.

____

____

____

2. What happened to the previous Receiver-in-Training?

____

____

____

3. How will Jonas spend his time as Receiver-in-Training?

____

____

____

4. Describe the Receiver's living space.

____

____

____

5. What does Jonas realize when he sees the books at the Receiver's dwelling?

____

____

____

____

6. How are Jonas and the Receiver to work together?

____

____

____

____

Name ____ Period ____________

The Giver
Quiz: Chapters 11-12

Directions: *For each of the following statements, write "true" if the statement is true and "false" if the statement is false. For each of the false statements, use the lines below the statement to rewrite the sentence, making the statement true.*

1. ___________Sailing on a lake is the first memory Jonas receives. ____________

   ____

2. ___________Jonas can change the things that occur in his memories. ________

   ____

3. ___________Snow, weather patterns, hills, and sunshine were eliminated when the community went to Sameness. ______________________________________

   ____

4. ___________Jonas is now to address his mentor as The Previous Receiver. ____

   ____

5. ___________Gabriel wakes up and fusses during the night. ________________

   ____

6. ___________Seeing Beyond means that Jonas can see what is occurring in communities outside of his own. _____________________________________

   ____

7. ___________The Giver has memories from many previous generations and of events outside of the community. ___________________________________

   ____

8. ___________The community's citizens can only see in white, red, and blue. ____

   ____

Name ______________________________________ Period ____________

The Giver
Vocabulary Quiz: Chapters 9-12

Directions: *Match the vocabulary words for numbers 1-8 with the correct definition from letters a-h. Then match the vocabulary words for numbers 9-16 with the correct definition from letters i-p. Write the letter of the correct definition on the line provided.*

1. ______	throng	a. source; beginning
2. ______	dismounting	b. large group of people
3. ______	relish	c. with fear or trepidation; suspiciously
4. ______	integral	d. necessary; essential
5. ______	origin	e. getting off something, such as a horse or bicycle
6. ______	alcove	f. one that follows another in a job or office
7. ______	successor	g. small recessed section of a room
8. ______	apprehensively	h. an appreciation of an experience; enjoyment

- -

9. ______	torrent	i. flinching away from pain
10. ______	glee	j. puzzled; confused
11. ______	obsolete	k. high-spirited joy
12. ______	wincing	l. buying and selling of goods
13. ______	commerce	m. flood; rapid outpouring
14. ______	admonition	n. cleverly; with humor and irony
15. ______	dumbfounded	o. no longer useful
16. ______	wryly	p. strong advice; warning

Name ____ Period ____________

The Giver
Quiz: Chapters 13-14

Directions: *CIRCLE the letter of the best answer for each of the following questions. WRITE the letter of the best choice on the lines provided at the bottom of the page.*

1. How and what colors does Jonas see?
   a. He sees flashes of blue.
   b. He sees red all the time.
   c. He sees flashes of red.
   d. He sees yellow all the time.

2. What does Jonas do after receiving the memory of the elephant?
   a. He tries to give a memory of the elephant to Lily.
   b. He researches a variety of animals.
   c. He visits the zoo.
   d. He gives Gabriel the memory of the elephant.

3. What happens in the memory of the elephant that Jonas receives?
   a. The elephant escapes from the zoo.
   b. The elephant bathes in a mud hole.
   c. The elephant is running on the African savanna.
   d. The elephant is poached and mourned by another elephant.

4. Which is *not* a reason why would it be difficult for the Receiver to be part of a family unit?
   a. He cannot tell anyone about his job.
   b. He has to travel a lot.
   c. He has to keep the books hidden from other citizens.
   d. He can only share the memories with the Receiver-in-Training.

5. How does Jonas's most recent sledding memory differ from the first one he received?
   a. Jonas uses a different type of sled.
   b. Jonas sleds down a different hill.
   c. Jonas falls off the sled and gets hurt.
   d. Jonas goes sledding with Lily.

6. Which of the Nurturers' standards has Gabriel not met?
   a. He has normal intelligence.
   b. He can sit alone.
   c. He has six teeth.
   d. He sleeps through the night.

7. Which of the following best describes Jonas's transmission of memory to Gabriel?
   a. Jonas never intentionally transmits a memory to Gabriel.
   b. Jonas gives Gabriel a soothing memory to help him sleep.
   c. Jonas gives Gabriel a memory of an elephant.
   d. Jonas gives Gabriel a memory of hunger.

1. _______ 2. _______ 3. _______ 4. _______ 5. _______ 6. _______ 7. _______

Name ____ Period ____________

The Giver
Quiz: Chapters 15-17

Directions: *Answer the following questions using complete sentences. Give as many details as possible to support your response.*

1. Contrast extended families in our society with extended families in the community.

____

____

____

2. Describe The Giver's favorite memory.

____

____

____

3. After receiving The Giver's favorite memory, what does Jonas tell Gabriel?

____

____

____

4. How is Jonas different after he stops taking his pills?

____

____

____

5. How does Jonas react when his friends play a war game?

____

____

____

6. What must Father do after the identical twins are born?

____

____

____

Name ____ Period ____________

The Giver
Vocabulary Quiz: Chapters 13-17

Directions: *Write the vocabulary word that best matches each definition, choosing from the word bank below. Be careful to spell the word correctly as you write. Not all words will be used.*

agony	anguish	assimilated	assuage
dejected	disengage	ecstatic	embedded
expertise	glum	injustice	irrationally
obsolete	ominous	permeated	placidly
sinuous	trudged	wisp	wry

1. foreboding sense of evil: ____
2. spread throughout; penetrated: ______________________________________
3. graceful and agile; full of smooth bends and curves: _______________________
4. mental pain, distress, or anxiety: ____________________________________
5. an integral part of something: ______________________________________
6. special skill or knowledge: ____
7. with a calm nature and appearance: ___________________________________
8. fragment; trace: ____
9. without reason or understanding: _____________________________________
10. dreary; gloomy: ____
11. intense pain: ____
12. unfair treatment: ____
13. to lessen the intensity of pain or discomfort; to calm: ______________________
14. feeling great pleasure or delight: ____________________________________
15. absorbed; understood: ____
16. walked steadily and with great effort: _________________________________

Name ____ Period ____________

The Giver
Quiz: Chapters 18-20

Directions: *For each of the following statements, write "true" if the statement is true and "false" if the statement is false. For each of the false statements, use the lines below the statement to rewrite the sentence, making the sentence true.*

1. ___________ Ten years ago, the rule that The Giver and Receiver-in-Training cannot request release was added. ____________________________________

____

2. ___________ Rosemary requested release from her Assignment and the community. ____

____

3. ___________ If Jonas disappeared, the memories would disappear with him.

____

____

4. ___________ The Giver tries to prevent Jonas from watching the video of the twin infant's release.____

____

5. ___________ Jonas's father kills the twin infant and puts its body in a box. ____

____

6. ___________ The Giver plans to flee from the community with Jonas. _______

____

7. ___________ The Giver first experienced hearing beyond instead of seeing beyond.

____

8. ___________ Jonas plans to escape the community by swimming across the river.

____

Name ____ Period ____________

The Giver
Quiz: Chapters 21-23

Directions: *Choose the best answer for each of the following questions. Write the letter of the correct answer on the lines provided at the bottom of the page.*

1. After seeing the video of the infant's release, Jonas
   a. spends the night at The Giver's dwelling
   b. confronts his father about the release
   c. runs away from The Giver's dwelling
   d. tells the citizens what really happens in a release

2. Why does Jonas not follow The Giver's escape plan?
   a. Jonas is angry at The Giver.
   b. Jonas has to flee earlier to escape his own release.
   c. Jonas must take Gabriel with him when he flees.
   d. Jonas cannot face his father after seeing the infant's release.

3. How does Jonas flee from the community?
   a. He steals The Giver's vehicle.
   b. He swims across the river.
   c. He stows away in a plane.
   d. He rides his father's bicycle.

4. How does the natural world change as Jonas and Gabriel get farther from the community?
   a. Jonas and Gabriel enter a war zone.
   b. Jonas and Gabriel see more animals and varied weather.
   c. Jonas and Gabriel enter a rain forest.
   d. Jonas and Gabriel see a large city.

5. What does Jonas find at the top of the hill?
   a. a sled
   b. a cell phone
   c. a direction sign
   d. a high wall

6. What does Jonas see and hear at the conclusion of the novel?
   a. the African savanna and an elephant bellowing
   b. a beach and pounding surf
   c. twinkling lights and singing
   d. a lake and whistling wind

1. ________ 2. ________ 3. ________ 4. ________ 5. ________ 6. ________

Name ______________________________ Period __________

The Giver
Vocabulary Quiz: Chapters 18-23

Directions: *Match the vocabulary words for numbers 1-8 with the correct definition from letters a-h. Then match the vocabulary words in number 9-16 with the correct definition from letters i-p. Write the letter of the correct definition on the line provided.*

1.	______	dejected	a. an idea occurring later
2.	______	excruciating	b. to get or obtain possession
3.	______	inflict	c. very unhappy; dispirited; disappointed
4.	______	afterthought	d. in a state of great hardship; miserable
5.	______	wretched	e. to cause or impose; to deal or mete out
6.	______	empowered	f. relief from emotional distress or grief
7.	______	acquire	g. gave authority or power to
8.	______	solace	h. extremely painful

- -

9.	______	churning	i. without energy; slow and sluggish
10.	______	rueful	j. slowed the progress of; interfered
11.	______	languid	k. splashing or turning violently
12.	______	augmented	l. made greater or more numerous
13.	______	vigilant	m. very heavy; like lead
14.	______	tantalizing	n. feeling, showing, or causing regret or pity
15.	______	impeded	o. teasing by showing something desirable but continually out of reach
16.	______	leaden	p. watchful and alert

Name ______________________________ Period ___________

The Giver
Final Test

Part A: Matching
Directions: *Match the following characters with the correct description or action. Write the letter of the correct answer on the line provided.*

1. ______ Jonas	a. Jonas's younger sister
2. ______ Father	b. newchild who does not sleep well at night
3. ______ Mother	c. assigned to be Assistant Director of Recreation
4. ______ Lily	d. previous Receiver-in-Training
5. ______ Asher	e. assigned to be the Receiver-in-Training
6. ______ Fiona	f. holds the community's memories
7. ______ Gabriel	g. lives at the House of the Old
8. ______ Giver	h. works as a Nurturer
9. ______ Rosemary	i. assigned as a Caretaker of the Old
10. ______ Larissa	j. works at the Department of Justice

Part B: True/False
Directions: *For each of the following statements, decide whether it is true or false. If true, write out the word "true" on the line provided; if false, write out the word "false."*

11. ____________ The male infant may be released because he cannot sit up on schedule.

12. ____________ Each December the children get a year older and gain new privileges and responsibilities.

13. ____________ Citizens are encouraged to be as similar to others as possible.

14. ____________ Citizens take a pill each day to make them stronger.

15. ____________ Newchildren are identified by a number before they are named.

16. ____________ The Receiver-in-Training will maintain his regular schedule and train after dinner each evening.

Name ____ Period ____________

The Giver—Final Test

17. ___________ Jonas's job is to receive all the world's memories from the current Receiver.

18. ___________ Sledding downhill is the first memory Jonas receives.

19. ___________ At first, Jonas can only see flashes of blue.

20. ___________ Jonas enjoys playing a war game with his friends.

21. ___________ Rosemary requested release to escape the pain of the memories.

22. ___________ Jonas takes Gabriel and Lily with him when he flees the community.

Part C: Multiple Choice
Directions: *Choose the letter of the best response. Write the letter of the correct answer on the line provided.*

23. ______ Which is NOT a reason that someone may be released?
    a. reward b. punishment
    c. infant not thriving d. elderly

24. ______ A Birthmother
    a. feeds her children b. has four children and then retires
    c. lives with her children d. has three children and then performs manual labor

25. ______ Which of the following is NOT provided for all citizens of the community?
    a. food b. a car
    c. medication d. a dwelling

26. ______ Who decides each Twelve's Assignment?
    a. the Twelve him/herself b. the Twelve's parents
    c. The Giver d. the Elders

27. ______ Which of the following is NOT a quality that the Receiver-in-Training must possess?
    a. Integrity b. Courage
    c. Sense of humor d. Capacity to See Beyond

28. ______ Which of the following is NOT a rule that Jonas must follow during his training?
    a. You may not lie. b. You may not participate in dream-telling.
    c. You may not apply for release. d. You may not discuss your training with anyone.

29. ______ Which of the following was NOT eliminated when the community went to Sameness?
    a. hills b. colors
    c. different types of food d. weather patterns

Name ____ Period ____________

The Giver—Final Test

30. ______ Gabriel has difficulty
    a. speaking clearly b. sitting up
    c. walking d. sleeping through the night

31. ______ The Giver's favorite memory is of
    a. walking on a beach b. a family at Christmas
    c. sledding downhill d. sailing on a lake

32. ______ Instead of seeing colors, The Giver first
    a. heard pounding surf b. saw glimpses of other communities
    c. heard music d. experienced different types of weather

33. ______ Which of the following is NOT true?
    a. Jonas protects Gabriel. b. Jonas misses his family unit.
    c. Jonas steals his father's bike. d. Jonas wants The Giver to leave the community.

Part D: Short Response (3-7 sentences each)
Directions: *Answer each of the following questions using complete sentences. Be sure to give as many details as possible to explain your answer to EACH question. Use a sheet of lined paper for your answers and staple it to the back page of your test.*

34. Explain how the community controls every aspect of the citizens' lives. Include specific examples from the novel in your answer.

35. How do Jonas's feelings about the community change from the beginning of the novel to the end? Use specific examples from the novel in your answer.

36. Contrast Jonas's relationship with his family unit to his relationship with The Giver.

Name ______________________________________ Period ____________

The Giver—Final Test

Part E: Vocabulary

Directions: *Match the following vocabulary words with the correct definition or synonym. Write the letter of the correct answer on the line provided.*

37. ______ ironic	a. to correct or punish
38. ______ aptitude	b. relating or applying to things that have happened in the past
39. ______ chastise	c. source; beginning
40. ______ reprieve	d. no longer useful
41. ______ meticulously	e. relief from emotional distress or grief
42. ______ retroactive	f. the opposite of intended or expected meaning
43. ______ benign	g. made greater or more numerous
44. ______ origin	h. absorbed; understood
45. ______ glee	i. natural ability
46. ______ obsolete	j. delay of punishment
47. ______ assimilated	k. unfair treatment
48. ______ injustice	l. high-spirited joy
49. ______ solace	m. very carefully; precisely
50. ______ augmented	n. mild; harmless

Name ____ Period ____________

The Giver
Final Test: Multiple Choice

Directions: *Circle the letter of the best response to each question. OR, if you have a separate answer sheet, fill in the bubble of the correct response on your answer document.*

Part A: Characters
Choose the letter of the BEST description for each character.

1. Jonas
   a. enjoys the community
   b. lives at the House of the Old
   c. assigned to be Receiver-in-Training
   d. cares for Gabriel

2. Father
   a. works as a Nurturer
   b. works in the Department of Justice
   c. always votes to keep Gabriel
   d. tries to leave the community

3. Mother
   a. works as a Nurturer
   b. works in the Department of Justice
   c. works at the House of the Old
   d. is friends with The Giver

4. Lily
   a. Jonas's older sister
   b. leaves the community with Jonas
   c. Jonas's younger sister
   d. does not like Gabriel

5. Asher
   a. Lily's friend
   b. Caretaker of the Old
   c. Assistant Director of Recreation
   d. drowns in the river

6. Fiona
   a. Assistant Director of Recreation
   b. Lily's best friend
   c. Mother's friend
   d. assigned as a Caretaker of the Old

7. Gabriel
   a. does not sleep well at night
   b. friend of Father's
   c. released by Father
   d. lives at the House of the Old

8. Giver
   a. agrees with the community's structures
   b. works with Mother
   c. does not get along with Jonas
   d. holds the community's memories

9. Rosemary
   a. Fiona's friend
   b. previous Receiver-in-Training
   c. works at the House of the Old
   d. holds the community's memories

10. Larissa
   a. works as a Nurturer
   b. The Giver's wife
   c. lives at the House of the Old
   d. Mother's friend

Part B: Plot
Choose the letter of the best response to each question.

11. What must families do at dinner each evening?
   a. tell the best and worst parts of their day
   b. make plans for the next day
   c. tell their feelings
   d. bless the food

12. Which is NOT a reason that someone may be released?
   a. reward
   b. punishment
   c. infant not thriving
   d. elderly

Name ______________________________________ Period __________

The Giver—Final Test: Multiple Choice

13. What happens each December?
    a. It snows.
    b. All children become a year older.
    c. Everyone goes on vacation.
    d. Everyone celebrates Christmas.

14. What does a Birthmother do?
    a. nurture newchildren
    b. raise children until they receive an Assignment
    c. gives birth three times, then performs hard labor the rest of her life
    d. acts as a grandmother to the community

15. Which of the following is NOT provided for all citizens of the community?
    a. food
    b. a car
    c. medication
    d. a dwelling

16. What new privilege do Eights earn?
    a. a bicycle
    b. a new sweater
    c. going on field trips
    d. performing volunteer hours

17. Before they are one year old, all newchildren
    a. live with foster families
    b. are given names
    c. begin to walk
    d. are identified by a number

18. Who decides each Twelve's Assignment?
    a. the Twelve him/herself
    b. the Twelve's parents
    c. The Giver
    d. the Elders

19. To select a Receiver-in-Training
    a. the community votes for an individual
    b. the previous Receiver selects him/her
    c. a person volunteers for the Assignment
    d. the Elders meticulously observe the students

20. Which of the following is NOT a quality that the Receiver-in-Training must possess?
    a. Integrity
    b. Courage
    c. Sense of humor
    d. Capacity to See Beyond

21. Which of the following is NOT a rule that Jonas must follow during his training?
    a. You may not lie.
    b. You may not participate in dream-telling.
    c. You may not apply for release.
    d. Do not discuss your training with anyone.

22. What happened to the previous Receiver-in-Training?
    a. She became the Chief Elder.
    b. Her name was designated Not-to-Be-Spoken.
    c. She ran away from the community.
    d. She resigned as Receiver-in-Training to take another Assignment.

Name ______________________________________ Period __________

The Giver—Final Test: Multiple Choice

23. How is Jonas supposed to address his mentor?
    a. The Previous Receiver b. Grandfather
    c. The Giver d. Sir
24. What is the first memory Jonas receives?
    a. the African savanna b. war
    c. sledding downhill d. a family at Christmas

25. Which of the following was NOT eliminated when the community went to Sameness?
    a. hills b. colors
    c. different types of food d. weather patterns

26. What is the first color can Jonas see?
    a. blue b. red
    c. green d. orange

27. Which of the following best describes Jonas's transmission of memory to Gabriel?
    a. Jonas never intentionally transmits a memory to Gabriel.
    b. Jonas gives Gabriel a soothing memory to help him sleep.
    c. Jonas gives Gabriel a memory of an elephant.
    d. Jonas gives Gabriel a memory of hunger.

28. Which of the Nurturers' standards has Gabriel NOT met?
    a. normal intelligence b. sitting up alone
    c. has six teeth d. sleeping through the night

29. The Giver's favorite memory is of
    a. walking on a beach b. a family at Christmas
    c. sledding downhill d. sailing on a lake

30. Instead of seeing colors, The Giver first
    a. heard pounding surf b. saw glimpses of other communities
    c. heard music d. experienced different types of weather

31. How does Jonas originally plan to escape from the community?
    a. in The Giver's vehicle b. swim across the river
    c. run across the bridge d. hide in an airplane

32. Which of the following is NOT true?
    a. Jonas protects Gabriel. b. Jonas misses his family unit.
    c. Jonas steals his Father's bike. d. Jonas wants The Giver to leave the community.

33. How does the natural world change as Jonas and Gabriel get farther from the community?
    a. Jonas and Gabriel enter a war zone.
    b. Jonas and Gabriel see animals and varied weather.
    c. Jonas and Gabriel enter a rain forest.
    d. Jonas and Gabriel see a large city.

Name ____ Period ____________

The Giver—Final Test: Multiple Choice

Part C: Vocabulary

Circle the letter of the best definition or synonym for each vocabulary word, OR fill in the bubble of the correct response on your answer sheet.

34. the opposite of intended or expected meaning
    a. ironic
    b. unanimous
    c. petulantly
    d. chastise
35. to correct or punish
    a. wheedle
    b. transgression
    c. avert
    d. chastise
36. relating or applying to things that have happened in the past
    a. profound
    b. embedded
    c. retroactive
    d. ominous
37. source; beginning
    a. origin
    b. leaden
    c. obsolete
    d. throng
38. no longer useful
    a. successor
    b. exuberant
    c. obsolete
    d. sinuous
39. unfair treatment of somebody
    a. indolence
    b. injustice
    c. disposition
    d. conviction
40. relief from emotional distress or grief
    a. agony
    b. permeated
    c. anguish
    d. solace
41. natural ability
    a. admonition
    b. expertise
    c. aptitude
    d. assimilated
42. delay of punishment
    a. reprieve
    b. conviction
    c. hasten
    d. admonition
43. mild; harmless
    a. rueful
    b. benign
    c. languid
    d. wisp
44. high-spirited joy
    a. palpable
    b. placid
    c. wryly
    d. glee
45. absorbed; understood
    a. empowered
    b. assimilated
    c. assuaged
    d. inflict
46. a large group of people
    a. alcove
    b. wisp
    c. throng
    d. commerce
47. meticulously; very carefully
    a. wryly
    b. scrupulously
    c. apprehensively
    d. petulantly
48. laziness; lack of interest
    a. disposition
    b. dismounting
    c. integral
    d. indolence
49. made greater or more numerous
    a. augmented
    b. profound
    c. palpable
    d. awed
50. one that follows another in a job or office
    a. emblem
    b. torrent
    c. vigilant
    d. successor

Teacher Guide
Summary of the Novel

Chapter One
It is December, and eleven-year-old Jonas feels uneasy as an unidentified aircraft flies over his community. All members of the community are ordered inside until the situation is rectified. At dinner with his family, Jonas confides that he is apprehensive about receiving his job Assignment at the upcoming Ceremony of Twelve.

Chapter Two
Jonas's father relates how he was placed in his job as Nurturer and tells the family unit about a newchild, Gabriel, who is not progressing well. Jonas's parents reassure him that the Elders of the community carefully observe each child before making his/her Assignment.

Chapter Three
In the hope that Gabriel will learn to sleep more soundly, Jonas's father receives permission to bring Gabriel to their family dwelling each night. Lily, Jonas's younger sister, looks forward to being an Eight, when she will begin her volunteer hours in the community. Later, when playing with his friend Asher, Jonas notices that Asher's apple has an unusual quality to it.

Chapter Four
Jonas helps bathe an elderly woman at the House of the Old. The woman, Larissa, tells Jonas that the home recently celebrated the release of Roberto, an elderly gentleman.

Chapter Five
During the morning sharing of dreams, Jonas recounts a dream in which he experienced sexual desire. His mother told him that these feelings are called Stirrings, and that Jonas must begin taking a pill each day to alleviate them.

Chapter Six
At the annual Naming and Placement Ceremony, newchildren are named and assigned to family units in the community. Lily becomes an Eight and receives her new jacket with a pocket. The Nines receive bicycles, and the Tens are given shorter haircuts. While waiting for the Ceremony of Twelve, Jonas and Asher discuss the care with which all decisions, including the Matching of Spouses, are made by the Elders.

Chapter Seven
At the Ceremony of Twelve, each youth's number is called and his/her Assignment is announced. Jonas's number is skipped, however, and he wonders what he has done wrong.

Chapter Eight
The Chief Elder informs the audience that Jonas has been selected to be the community's next Receiver of Memory. The crowd is informed that the Receiver must possess Intelligence, Integrity, Courage, Wisdom, and the Capacity to See Beyond. While looking at the crowd, Jonas again notices a fleeting change, as he had previously when viewing the apple.

Chapter Nine
Jonas learns that the community chose a Receiver ten years previously, but that her name is now designated Not-to-Be-Spoken. When reading the instructions for his Assignment, Jonas is shocked to learn that he is exempted from rules governing rudeness and that he may now lie.

Chapter Ten
When Jonas reports for his first day of training, he is amazed to see a luxurious room full of books and realizes that The Giver may turn off his speaker which monitors all buildings in the community. Jonas learns that he is supposed to receive all the memories of the world from the previous Receiver. By placing his hands on Jonas's bare back, the elderly gentleman transmits to Jonas a memory of riding on a sled.

Chapter Eleven
Even though he has no knowledge of snow, Jonas enjoys sledding down a hill. The previous Receiver, who is now The Giver, tells Jonas that snow and hills used to exist before the community went to Climate Control and Sameness.

Chapter Twelve
Jonas learns that he saw glimpses of colors, a type of seeing beyond, in the apple and the audience's faces at the Ceremony. Due to Sameness, colors no longer exist in the community. Jonas is excited to learn that he will be able to see more colors as he gains more memories from The Giver.

Chapter Thirteen
The Giver transmits to Jonas the memory of an elephant being slaughtered, and Jonas realizes that real elephants, not just stuffed ones like Lily's Comfort Object, once existed. The Giver tells Jonas that his life as the Receiver of Memory will be a solitary one. The books in The Giver's office, as well as the memories he possesses, may not be shared with anyone else in the community. The Elders may call on The Giver when they need counsel or advice, but that will occur only rarely. Jonas begins to wonder if the visions in his dreams—hills, snow, animals—still exist outside of the community.

Chapter Fourteen
As part of his training, Jonas must also receive memories that involve pain. Jonas relates his frustration that he alone must bear the memories for everyone, when it would be easier if the burden was shared among all citizens of the community. Later that night when Gabriel sleeps fitfully, Jonas transmits a memory of a tranquil lake to Gabriel to calm him.

Chapter Fifteen
The Giver transmits a gruesome battle scene to Jonas and apologizes for doing so.

Chapter Sixteen
The Giver transmits his favorite memory, a loving family at Christmas, to Jonas. Jonas is confused by the grandparents in the memory since elderly people are not involved in family units in the community. When Jonas asks his father if he loves him that evening, he is hurt when his father remarks that love is an imprecise word for an obsolete feeling. Jonas begins

to transmit pleasant memories to Gabriel each night and yearns for a world in which love is not obsolete. Jonas secretly stops taking his daily pill.

Chapter Seventeen
As a result of no longer taking the pills, Jonas sees everything in color and experiences a greater depth of feelings, a fact which alienates Jonas from his age-mates. Gabriel has begun to walk and, thus, must also endure being reprimanded with a discipline wand. Jonas's father comments that a set of twins will be born the next day, and he will select the twin to keep in the community and the twin to release to Elsewhere.

Chapter Eighteen
The Giver tells Jonas that the Elders selected a Receiver of Memory, Rosemary, ten years ago. After receiving many emotionally painful memories, Rosemary requested release. When this occurred, the memories that she possessed were released into the community and caused great despair.

Chapter Nineteen
Anticipating a joyful event, Jonas asks to watch his father perform the Release Ceremony for one of the twins. Jonas is shocked when he sees his father euthanize the smaller twin and place his dead body in a box.

Chapter Twenty
Jonas is horrified to realize that people who are released are actually killed, not taken to live Elsewhere. The Giver realizes that life in the community must change, and he tells Jonas of his plan to release Jonas's memories into the community. The Giver will help Jonas escape from the community, and The Giver will remain behind to help the community process and learn from the memories. Jonas also learns that Rosemary was The Giver's daughter.

Chapter Twenty-One
At the evening meal, Jonas's father tells the family that Gabriel will be released since he is still not sleeping through the night. Disregarding the escape plan he made with The Giver, Jonas sneaks Gabriel out of his family's dwelling that night. While evading search planes, Jonas rides his father's bicycle with Gabriel out of the community and continues to ride for several days.

Chapter Twenty-Two
As Jonas and Gabriel move farther away from the community, the landscape begins to change and animals appear. They experience rain for the first time, and Jonas struggles to find food and shelter for himself and Gabriel.

Chapter Twenty-Three
As it begins to snow, Jonas and Gabriel trudge up a steep hill where Jonas finds a sled. They ride the sled down the hill toward a town full of twinkling colored lights. Jonas hears music and singing for the first time, which was The Giver's first experience with Hearing/Seeing Beyond.

Vocabulary with Definitions

Chapters One-Two
1. ironic (2)- the opposite of intended or expected meaning
2. palpable (3)- noticeable; intense; obvious
3. wheedle (5)- to influence someone through flattery or trickery
4. disposition (7)- personality; attitude
5. transgression (9)- breaking a law or rule
6. awed (12)- brought up feelings of amazement or fear
7. technically (13)- strictly; based on legal interpretation
8. aptitude (15)- natural ability

Chapters Three-Four
1. chastise (20)- to correct or punish
2. petulantly (22)- in a touchy, sullen, or grumpy manner
3. remorse (23)- a strong feeling of guilt or regret
4. conviction (24)- belief
5. hasten (27)- move or act quickly
6. tabulated (28)- calculated
7. nuisance (30)- annoying or irritating; unpleasant
8. chortled (33)- laughed; giggled

Chapters Five-Six
1. disquieting (34)- causing a feeling of anxiety; disturbing
2. emblem (41)- something that visually symbolizes an object, idea, group, or quality; a symbol
3. reprieve (42)- delay of punishment
4. relinquish (42)- to give up; surrender
5. exuberant (44)- full of enthusiasm; lively
6. infringed (45)- intruded upon land, rights, or privileges that belong to someone else
7. meticulously (48)- very carefully and precisely
8. scrupulously (48)- meticulously; very carefully

Chapters Seven-Eight
1. profound (51)- deep, strong, or intense
2. prestige (53)- high standing in others' opinions
3. retroactive (54)- relating or applying to things that have happened in the past
4. avert (57)- to turn away
5. benign (59)- mild; harmless
6. indolence (61)- laziness; lack of interest
7. unanimous (61)- all members of a group in complete agreement
8. spontaneously (64)- occurring naturally, without being planned

Chapters Nine-Ten
1. throng (65)- large group of people
2. dismounting (66)- getting off something, such as a horse or bicycle
3. relish (68)- appreciation; enjoyment
4. integral (70)- necessary; essential
5. origin (73)- source; beginning
6. alcove (74)- small recessed section of a room
7. successor (76)- one that follows another in a job or office
8. apprehensively (79)- with fear or trepidation; suspiciously

Chapters Eleven-Twelve
1. torrent (81)- flood; rapid outpouring
2. glee (82)- high-spirited joy
3. obsolete (84)- no longer useful
4. wincing (86)- flinching away from pain
5. commerce (89)- buying and selling of goods
6. admonition (89)- strong advice; warning
7. dumbfounded (93)- puzzled; confused
8. wryly (95)- cleverly; with humor and irony

Chapters Thirteen-Fourteen

1. irrationally (99)- without reason or understanding
2. sinuous (100)- graceful and agile; full of smooth bends and curves
3. assimilated (104)- absorbed; understood
4. embedded (106)- an integral part of something
5. agony (109)- intense pain
6. assuage (110)- to lessen the intensity of pain or discomfort; to calm
7. ominous (113)- foreboding sense of evil
8. placidly (114)- with a calm nature and appearance

Chapters Fifteen-Seventeen

1. anguish (118)- mental pain, distress, or anxiety
2. ecstatic (122)- feeling great pleasure or delight
3. wisp (125)- fragment; trace
4. permeated (131)- spread throughout; penetrated
5. injustice (132)- unfair treatment
6. expertise (134)- special skill or knowledge
7. trudged (135)- walk steadily and with great effort
8. glum (136)- dreary; gloomy

Chapters Eighteen-Twenty

1. dejected (139)- very unhappy; dispirited; disappointed
2. excruciating (140)- extremely painful
3. inflict (142)- to cause or impose; to deal or mete out
4. afterthought (146)- an idea occurring later
5. wretched (151)- in a state of great hardship; miserable
6. empowered (153)- gave authority or power to
7. acquire (156)- to get or obtain possession
8. solace (161)- relief from emotional distress or grief

Chapters Twenty-One—Twenty-Three

1. churning (163)- splashing or turning violently
2. rueful (164)- feeling, showing or causing regret or pity
3. languid (166)- without energy; slow and sluggish
4. augmented (168)- made greater or more numerous
5. vigilant (169)- watchful and alert
6. tantalizing (172)- teasing by showing something desirable but continually out of reach
7. impeded (176)- slowed the progress of; interfered
8. leaden (177)- very heavy; like lead

Pre-Reading Ideas and Activities
Suggested activities prior to the study of *The Giver:*

1. Record an interview with one of your grandparents. Ask him (her) to share a favorite memory with you. Ask him to also share any stories that one of his parents shared with him. If you are not able to interview a grandparent, visit a retirement center and interview one of the residents.
2. Discuss what it would be like to live in a society where citizens do not have the freedom to choose their spouse, occupation, etc. How would your life be different from what it is now? How would your expectations of the future differ?
3. Research societies where citizens do not have freedom of choice, such as Communist China, the former Soviet Union, Communist Cuba. Create a Venn diagram comparing and contrasting their lives to the life of a person living in the United States.
4. Learn about genetics and Gregor Mendel. Which traits are dominant and recessive? Create tables to demonstrate the inheritance of traits for blue/brown eyes, red/blond hair, height, racial traits, etc.
5. Select several modern-day cultures which differ greatly from your own. Work individually or in small groups to learn more about them. Create a short oral report of the information that you learn and share it with the class.
6. As a class, create a future world. In small groups, create different aspects of the society such as transportation, home life, government, food supplies, security, education. (You may want to place restrictions on the society such as severe drought, civil unrest, or war.)
7. Write a brief narrative in which a main character must choose between his (her) personal beliefs and his family. Be sure to include the emotions the character experiences as he struggles to make a decision.
8. Read several magazine articles about predictions for future technology or impending world issues. Create a poster detailing the technology or possible future international issues.
9. Brainstorm rites of passage (starting school, driver's license, first date, and many more) in our society. What determines when these rites of passage of occur? Do they occur at the same time for everyone? Should they occur at the same time for everyone? Why or why not?
10. Write an essay describing a grown person whom you *personally* know and admire. Include the reasons why you respect and admire this person and the effect he/she has had on your personality and life. (You may wish to place restrictions on the type of person, such as prohibiting sports figures, musicians, movie stars, etc.)
11. Read a novel which is set in a future society: *The City of Ember* by DuPrau (2003), *Brave New World* by Huxley (1932), *1984* by Orwell (1949), *Fahrenheit 451* by Bradbury (1953). Write 2-3 paragraphs about how the society changes from the beginning to the end of the book.
12. Read another novel by Lois Lowry: *Number the Stars* (1989), *Gossamer* (2006), *A Summer to Die* (1977), *Autumn Street* (1980). Write 2-3 paragraphs summarizing the novel.
13. Read a science fiction novel: *A Wrinkle in Time* by L'Engle (1962), *Journey to the Center of the Earth* by Verne (1870), *The Invisible Man* by Wells (1897), *Frankenstein* by Shelley (1818), *Foundation* by Asimov (1951). Write 2-3 paragraphs summarizing the novel.
14. Listen to a radio broadcast of *The War of the Worlds* or watch a science fiction movie such as *A Wrinkle in Time* or *The Matrix.* Discuss the elements of science fiction in the work you chose.

Post-Reading Extension Activities and Alternative Assessment

The following are suggested activities to supplement the study of ***The Giver*** *after reading the novel. Activities can be presented in any form.*

Cross-Curricular Activities (Multiple Subjects)

1. Write and stage a presentation to the Elders in which Jonas and The Giver lobby to have memories made available to all citizens.
2. Assume that Jonas and Gabriel reach an outside world similar to a society that currently exists. Write a newspaper article about Jonas and Gabriel doing so. Also write a series of letters to a newspaper discussing whether that society should intervene in the community. Be sure to write letters with varying viewpoints.
3. Make a poster or brochure about the life and work of Lois Lowry. Include information about major events in her life, her major works, and how her life has influenced her writing.

Art

1. Create a map of the community. Use details from the novel to accurately create your map.
2. Create a book jacket for the novel. The book jacket must have an original picture on the front cover that represents the novel and a summary of the novel on the back cover. Also include an author biography and critic's review of the novel on the inside flaps.

Literature

1. Revisit the predictions you made on pages 22, 24, and 25 after reading Chapters One and Two. Assess which predictions were accurate and which ones were not.
2. Read one of the other books in Lowry's *The Giver* trilogy. After reading *Gathering Blue* and/or *Messenger*, write an essay comparing and contrasting it to *The Giver*.

Science/Technology

1. Create a poster or other visual display of technology that you believe would exist in the community. Be sure to include specific examples from the novel, such as technology used to decide weather patterns and eliminate colors.
2. Imagine that you are a psychologist in the outside world assigned to evaluate Jonas after he escapes from the community. Create a medical file discussing Jonas's psychological and emotional health. Include any issues or problems that Jonas must deal with, as well as how he is coping with the outside world.

History

1. Research a society which has undergone a drastic change in government, such as the Russian Revolution, China's Communist takeover, the French Revolution, the fall of the Berlin Wall, or the American Revolution. Learn about how the society and new government dealt with the changes. Present your findings in an oral report to the class.
2. Analyze human rights in the context of the novel. How does the community's human rights record compare to human rights in our society? Also examine the role of women in the community, as compared to our society. Present your findings and opinions in an oral or written report.

Essay/Writing Ideas

For this Guide, essay and writing activities are two different types of writing assignments. For the essay ideas, be sure to answer the questions in a succinct, comprehensive, five-paragraph essay. Each answer should be at least 2-3 typed, double-spaced pages. Writing activities are those that do not necessarily follow the "essay" format. For the writing ideas, follow the directions given.

Essay Ideas

1. George Santayana said, "Those who cannot remember the past are condemned to repeat it." Discuss how this holds true in *The Giver*. Include specific examples from the novel in your answer.
2. Compare and contrast the Assignment of Receiver to another real (such as a history book) or imagined (such as the pensieve in Harry Potter books) container of memories.
3. Much of Jonas's decision to leave the community centered on Gabriel. How do you think Jonas would have performed his Assignment if Gabriel had not been in the novel? Would Jonas still have fled the community or would he have stayed? Include reasons to support your answer.
4. Analyze the character of The Giver. What is his role in the story? Why is the novel named after him and not Jonas? How does his role change?
5. Write an essay which agrees or disagrees with the following statement: The community's structure and the Elders' control depended on secrecy and the citizens not revealing the truth about their Assignments. Include specific examples from the novel to support your answer.

Writing Ideas

1. Write a sequel to *The Giver* which tells what happens to Jonas and Gabriel in the future.
2. Write a sequel to *The Giver* which tells what happens to the community in the future.
3. Write an essay describing your favorite memory and how it could have been included in the novel.
4. Jonas wonders what words one could use to describe the experience of sunshine. Describe sunshine in a poem or descriptive paragraph.
5. *The Giver* is presented from Jonas's point of view. Rewrite a portion of the book from his father or mother's point of view.
6. Write a narrative which occurs in a dystopian society. Be sure to include how the citizens become disenchanted with the perceived perfection of their society.
7. Imagine that you live in the community. Create a series of journal entries about your life. Include the name you are given, information about your family unit, how you cope with each year's new responsibilities, where you perform your volunteer hours, your Assignment, how you feel about your Assignment, and what you do as you grow older.
8. Jonas does not confront his father about the infant's release. Write and act out a scene in which Jonas does choose to discuss the infant's and Gabriel's impending release with his father.
9. Rewrite the ending of *The Giver*. You may veer from the novel at any point in the story.

Project Rubric

Category	*Score of 4*	*Score of 3*	*Score of 2*	*Score of 1*
Required Elements **SCORE _____**	Includes all required elements as stated in directions	Includes all but one required element as stated in directions	Missing 2-3 of the required elements as stated in the directions	Missing 4 or more of the elements as stated in the directions
Graphics and Illustrations **SCORE _____**	All pictures and graphics are appropriate and enhance the project	Some pictures and graphics are included which enhance the project	Few pictures or graphics are included which enhance the project	No pictures or graphics are included which enhance the project
Creativity **SCORE _____**	Exceptionally clever and unique approach to the project	Clever at times; thoughtfully and uniquely presented	A few original touches enhance the project	Shows little creativity, originality, and/ or effort
Neatness and Attractiveness **SCORE _____**	Exceptionally neat and attractive design and layout	Neat and attractive design and layout	Acceptably attractive, but a bit messy at times	Unattractive and messy; work shows no pride or effort
Grammar, Spelling, Mechanics **SCORE _____**	No grammatical, spelling, or punctuation mistakes in the project	A few grammatical, spelling, or punctuation mistakes which do not distract from the project	Several grammatical, spelling, or punctuation mistakes which distract from the project	Many grammatical, spelling, or punctuation mistakes in the project
Overall Effectiveness **SCORE _____**	Engaging project which captures the interest of the audience; shows great sense of pride and effort	Well done and interesting; shows sense of pride and effort	Interesting at times; logically organized; shows some sense of pride and effort	Not organized; does not hold the audience's attention; shows little or no pride or effort in work

Final Score: ____________ out of 24

Comments: ____

____

Response to Literature Rubric

Adapted from the **California Writing Assessment Rubric**
California Department of Education, Standards and Assessment Division

Score of 4

- ☐ Clearly addresses all parts of the writing task.
- ☐ Provides a meaningful thesis and thoughtfully supports the thesis and main ideas with facts, details, and/or explanations.
- ☐ Maintains a consistent tone and focus and a clear sense of purpose and audience.
- ☐ Illustrates control in organization, including effective use of transitions.
- ☐ Provides a variety of sentence types and uses precise, descriptive language.
- ☐ Contains few, if any, errors in the conventions of the English language (grammar, punctuation, capitalization, spelling). These errors do not interfere with the reader's understanding of the writing.
- ☐ Demonstrates a *clear* understanding of the ambiguities, nuances, and complexities of the text.
- ☐ Develops interpretations that demonstrate a thoughtful, comprehensive, insightful grasp of the text, and supports these judgments with specific references to various texts.
- ☐ Draws well-supported inferences about the effects of a literary work on its audience.
- ☐ Provides *specific* textual examples and/or personal knowledge and details to support the interpretations and inferences.

Score of 3

- ☐ Addresses all parts of the writing task.
- ☐ Provides a thesis and supports the thesis and main ideas with mostly relevant facts, details, and/or explanations.
- ☐ Maintains a generally consistent tone and focus and a general sense of purpose and audience.
- ☐ Illustrates control in organization, including *some* use of transitions.
- ☐ Includes a variety of sentence types and *some* descriptive language.
- ☐ Contains some errors in the conventions of the English language. These errors do not interfere with the reader's understanding of the writing.
- ☐ Develops interpretations that demonstrate a comprehensive grasp of the text and supports these interpretations with references to various texts.
- ☐ Draws supported inferences about the effects of a literary work on its audience.
- ☐ Supports judgments with some specific references to various texts and/or personal knowledge.
- ☐ Provides textual examples and details to support the interpretations.

Score of 2

- ☐ Addresses *only parts* of the writing task.
- ☐ *Suggests* a central idea with *limited* facts, details, and/or explanation.
- ☐ Demonstrates *little* understanding of purpose and audience.
- ☐ Maintains an *inconsistent* point of view, focus, and/or organizational structure which may include *ineffective or awkward* transitions that do not unify important ideas.
- ☐ Contains *several errors* in the conventions of the English language. These errors may interfere with the reader's understanding of the writing.
- ☐ Develops interpretations that demonstrate a limited grasp of the text.
- ☐ Includes interpretations that *lack* accuracy or coherence as related to ideas, premises, or images from the literary work.
- ☐ Draws *few* inferences about the effects of a literary work on its audience.
- ☐ Supports judgments with *few, if any*, references to various text and/or personal knowledge.

Score of 1

- ☐ Addresses *only one* part of the writing task.
- ☐ *Lacks* a thesis or central idea but may contain *marginally related* facts, details, and/or explanations.
- ☐ Demonstrates *no* understanding of purpose and audience.
- ☐ *Lacks* a clear point of view, focus, organizational structure, and transitions that unify important ideas.
- ☐ Includes *no* sentence variety; sentences are simple.
- ☐ Contains *serious errors* in the conventions of the English language. These errors interfere with the reader's understanding of the writing.
- ☐ Develops interpretations that demonstrate *little* grasp of the text.
- ☐ *Lacks* an interpretation or *may* be a simple retelling of the text.
- ☐ *Lacks* inferences about the effects of a literary work on its audience.
- ☐ *Fails* to support judgments with references to various text and/or personal knowledge.
- ☐ *Lacks* textual examples and details.

Answer Key

Note: Answers may not be given in complete sentences, as most student answers should be.

Page 10: Standards Focus: Exploring Expository Writing—Author Biography

1. c. to provide information about Lois Lowry
2. d. none of the above
3. b. It influenced her writing of *The Giver*.
4. a. in paragraph six
5. *Number the Stars* in 1989, *The Giver* in 1993
6. a particular category or type of writing; realistic fiction, historical fiction, and fantasy; *A Summer to Die* was realistic fiction, *Number the Stars* was historical fiction, *The Giver* was a fantasy

Page 12: Standards Focus: Exploring Expository Writing—Genre

1. c. setting the novel in a "lost world"
2. b. *Wizard of Oz*
3. c. The novel occurs in a realistic setting.
4. d. The author does not state his/her opinion of science fiction.
5. A utopian society takes place in a perfect world in which everyone is personally fulfilled. In a dystopian society, the culture's ideals have been taken too far and are dangerous to the society's inhabitants.
6. Fantasy novels take place in an imaginary world in which magic and supernatural powers are present. Science fiction novels also occur in an imaginary world, but the novel deals more with the impact that science and technology have on humans and their daily existence. Science fiction is a subgenre of fantasy. All science fiction novels are classified as fantasy, but not all fantasy novels are science fiction.

Pages 17-19: Anticipation/Reaction Guide and Reflection

Answers are personal and will vary.

Page 22: Note-Taking and Summarizing: Chapter 2

Each chapter has at least one page for this activity. See *Summary of the Novel* (pgs. 111-113) for possible answers. *Student answers will always vary.*

Page 23: Comprehension Check: Chapters 1-2 *Answers will vary*

Chapter One

1. Answers may include security or safety issues.
2. Pilot, Street Cleaner, Landscape Worker, Food Delivery, Speaker, Nurturer, Department of Justice
3. The citizens are instructed to leave their bicycles where they are and to go inside. The Pilot will be released.
4. Asher must publicly apologize to his class with a standard apology phrase. *Answers will vary.*
5. Answers should include a lack of individuality and the requirement of sharing thoughts and feelings so that no one has secrets.
6. Children who are eleven and seven years old, respectively; in this society, children are identified as a group
7. Answers may include family having dinner together, rather than a nightly telling of feelings.
8. Lily uses "animals" to describe people who don't fit in because she has not seen animals like we have.
9. A Nurturer is similar to an infant nurse and daycare worker.
10. He is not sleeping soundly at night.
11. Punishment, being elderly, and an infant not thriving.
12. Spouses are assigned, and each family unit has a boy and a girl.
13. It is against the rules to keep your feelings hidden. *Answers will vary*

Chapter Two

1. In Jonas's society, everyone becomes a year older and experiences the yearly Ceremony in December. Our society celebrates several religious holidays in December.
2. At the Ceremony of the Ones, the fifty children who were born that year become a One and are given names. It is odd for everyone born within 12 months with varied development stages to all turn one at the same time.

3. A family unit applies for a child when they are ready. Each family receives only one boy and one girl child. The mothers are not pregnant; all families are created through adoption, not biology.
4. Infants live at a childcare center and are not given names until they are one. This does not allow infants to form a close bond with their parents and could inhibit them developmentally.
5. Father finds out Gabriel's name so he can call him by name when they are alone together.
6. The rule about not riding bicycles until age nine is frequently broken.
7. Rules can only be changed by a committee, and this rarely occurs.
8. The Receiver
9. The Committee of Elders observes and receives input about each Eleven from their teachers. At the Ceremony of Twelve, each person's lifetime Assignment is announced.
10. Citizens have very little recourse to change their Assignments. *Answers will vary.*
11. Birthdays are not celebrated because there is no room for individuality. Since the point of growing up is to hold a job and contribute to the community, age is not important after jobs are assigned to Twelves.
12. Answers should include that it occurs at some time in the future. It could not occur in a democratic society, but some aspects of the society could possibly happen in a Communist society or in a new society created after cataclysmic world events such as a nuclear holocaust, highly destructive war, etc.

Pages 24-25: Standards Focus: Foreshadowing

Answers will vary. Students should try to discern what may occur as far as plot, character change, conflict, etc. Sample student answers are given.

1. Jonas will be put in a new situation where he doesn't know the rules and feels strange and stupid.
2. Release of elderly and newchildren will occur in the novel.
3. Jonas will have to confront the release of someone he is close to.
4. Gabriel will be slated for release.
5. Jonas will meet the Receiver.
6. Jonas will not have as close a relationship with his friends as he currently enjoys.
7. Jonas will be troubled by his Assignment.

Pages 26-27: Assessment Preparation: Punctuation, Capitalization, Spelling, and Grammar *Corrections are underlined*

1. There was an ironic tone to that final message, as if the Speaker found it amusing; and Jonas had smiled a little, though he knew what a grim statement it had been.
2. Now, thinking about the feeling of fear as he pedaled home along the river path, he remembered that moment of palpable, stomach-sinking terror when the aircraft had streaked above.
3. “Male,” Father said. “He's a sweet little male with a lovely disposition.”
4. “I feel frightened, too, for him” she confessed. “You know that there's ~~not~~ no third chance. The rules say that if there's a third transgression, he simply has to be released.”
5. It didn't seem a terribly important rule, but the fact that his father had broken a rule at all awed him.
6. “All the things I do with my friends,” Jonas pointed out, and his mother nodded in agreement.
7. For a contributing citizen to be released from the community was a final decision, a terrible punishment, an overwhelming statement of failure.
8. “I apologize for inconveniencing my learning community.” Asher ran through the standard apology phrase rapidly, still catching his breath.
9. “Why do you think the visitors didn't obey the rules?” Mother asked.
10. “I'm feeling apprehensive,” he confessed, glad that the appropriate descriptive word had finally come to him.

Pages 28-29: Note-Taking and Summarizing: Chapters 3-4

Each chapter has at least one page for this activity. See *Summary of the Novel* (pgs. 111-113) for possible answers. *Student answers will always vary.*

Page 30: Comprehension Check: Chapters 3-4 *Answers will vary*

Chapter Three

1. Answers may include environmental reasons, to minimize the community's need for fuel, compared to cars; makes it difficult to escape the community
2. pale eyes
3. Pale eyes are a genetic trait that is uncommon in the community. Jonas and Gabriel are probably biologically related.
4. unintelligent, lower class, not an Assignment that most women want to receive, allowed 3 births then do manual labor, just used for births, not assigned a family unit, looked down on by others
5. Citizens want to be as similar to others as possible. Individuality is not expressed or shown, and one does not draw attention to any form of individuality in himself or others.
6. to prevent the Birthmothers from forming a bond with the newchildren or experiencing any maternal feelings; Birthmothers are not viewed as actual parents.
7. He notices something different about the apple and wants to investigate it more.
8. to improve Asher's below-standard hand-eye coordination
9. Answers should include feeding, sleeping through the night, and diaper changes
10. American families usually have evening activities such as homework, sports practices, music lessons, scouts, etc. The community families just spend quiet evenings at home.

Chapter Four

1. The community's goal is not to ensure a pleasant childhood, but to create workers for the community. All Assignments serve the community, not private businesses.
2. Answers might include that people should not brag, but the community's rule against it intervenes in one's private life too much.
3. Food, clothing, home, job, bicycles for transportation, elder care, education, childcare
4. At the Ceremony of Twelve individual talents are taken into account, each child's Assignment is announced individually, and he/she is applauded. At a release of an elderly Person, the person's life is told, he/she is toasted, and individual speeches are made about him/her. Both have a party-like atmosphere.
5. Answers will probably include a place where Jonas has done volunteer hours such as the Recreation Area or House of the Old.
6. Neither lives with a family, are allowed to care for themselves, have their modesty respected, or are allowed privacy. They are both bathed by others and not permitted to make decisions for themselves.
7. *Answers will vary*

Pages 31-32: Standards Focus: Point of View

Answers will vary. Sample student answers are given.

1. "Jonas turned to the school assignments on his desk. Some chance of *that,* he thought. Lily was *never* quiet. Probably she should hope for an Assignment as Speaker, so that she could sit in the office with the microphone all day, making announcements."
2. A Birthmother probably feels that her Assignment is important. The society continues to grow with new citizens because of the Birthmothers.
3. a) He wanted to investigate what he saw happening to the apple. b) *Answers are personal and will vary.*
4. *Answers will vary.* Since this society has been conditioned to think a certain way, Larissa probably thinks nothing of Jonas bathing her. She probably does feel safe because she is being taken care of, unlike what can happen in our society, when some old people are put in retirement homes and forgotten.
5. *Answers are personal and will vary.*

Pages 33-34: Assessment Preparation: Word Origins—Etymology

Answers b. and d. will vary. Part c. dictionary definition is below.

1. insolent or rude in speech or behavior
2. a gnawing distress arising from a sense of guilt for past wrongs; feelings of guilt
3. a firmly held belief; the act of finding someone guilty of a crime
4. to do something immediately; speed up
5. to count, record, or list systematically

6. annoying, unpleasant, or obnoxious
7. a noisy, gleeful laugh

Pages 35-36: Note-Taking and Summarizing: Chapters 5-6
Each chapter has at least one page for this activity. See *Summary of the Novel* (pgs. 111-113) for possible answers. *Student answers will always vary.*

Page 37: Comprehension Check: Chapters 5-6 *Answers will vary*
Chapter Five
1. to find out what emotions each citizen is experiencing and to monitor them so that they don't do or think about anything unusual or forbidden
2. Both dreams deal with security guards and punishment, so Lily and Mother probably fear the community's rules and methods of punishment.
3. Mothers exist purely as part of a family unit. They probably do not have the option to stay home because the text says that all children go to the Childcare Center during the day to ensure that all children are raised the same.
4. It decreases emotional ties within families and makes families purely utilitarian to raise children to serve the community.
5. He has hit puberty and is developing feelings for girls.
6. Larissa- relaxing, gentle, grandmotherly, purpose of cleaning; Fiona- experiences desire, purpose of personal enjoyment
7. Answers will probably include feeling embarrassed or violated. You should be able to keep your feelings and dreams private.
8. Drugs them into submission, diminishes any feelings of desire, birth control since children are only born through Birthmothers
9. Feeling emotions would upset the detached quality of relationships. People might want to create families on their own with a chosen spouse and biological children.
10. They were pleasurable, and he would like to experience them again.

Chapter Six
1. The Ceremony for each year of change for the children
2. Children stay with others of their own age. Youth and adults work in Assignment groups. Elderly stay as a group in House of the Old.
3. *Answers will vary.* Students' reasons should logically support the proposed change.
4. Probably with a family's personal care
5. Ceremony of Loss- community murmurs the name of the "lost" all day with their voices gradually getting softer; Murmur-of-Replacement Ceremony- community murmurs the name of the child over time and it gradually grows louder
6. Only having one name at a time implies individuality in a society that does not support individuality.
7. *Answers will vary*
8. *Answers will vary*
9. *Answers will vary*
10. Answers may include different personality types, the disabled, etc.
11. Jonas is confident that his Assignment will be the right one for him. He has been conditioned to believe that the Elders know what is best for him.

Pages 38-39: Standards Focus: Symbolism
Ones: Receives name and placed with a family—now part of the community
Fours-Sixes: Jacket that buttons in the back—learn interdependence
Sevens: Jacket that buttons in the front—first visible sign of growing up
Eights: Jacket with smaller buttons and a pocket—can take care of own belongings; Comfort object taken away—should be able to soothe self ; Begin volunteer hours—old enough to show personal responsibility
Nines: Girls remove hair ribbons—no longer a little girl; Get bicycles—moving out into the community and away from the family
Tens: Girls braids are cut and boys get short haircuts—now a young adult and no longer a child
Elevens: Different undergarments for girls and longer pants for boys with a calculator pocket—bodies are changing and maturing, also doing more complicated schoolwork
Twelves: Receive job Assignment—now a contributing member of the community, no longer a child

Gabriel was the angel who predicted Jesus's birth. Gabriel in the novel serves as a catalyst to save Jonas from the community and its structures.

Our Society: Answers may vary depending upon the students' upbringing and culture. Sample student answers are given.

Birth: given a name and family—now a part of community and family

Four or Five: Begin kindergarten—beginning of school career

Thirteen: no longer a child; now considered a "teenager"—expected to begin puberty and the process of maturing into a young adult

Fifteen or Sixteen: many students will respond with a Quincinera, an important coming of age for a girl in Latin cultures; "Sweet Sixteen"—a coming of age for girls in the U.S.; often both boys and girls will get their driver's license at this time; some kids begin dating at fifteen or sixteen

Eighteen: able to vote, graduate, enlist in the military, and go to college or work—significant coming of age milestone, legally considered an adult in the U.S.

Twenty-One: legal age to be able to drink alcohol in most parts of the U.S.—an important milestone of the "last" of the milestones for young adults. *Answers will vary.*

Pages 40-41: Assessment Preparation: Identifying Parts of Speech

1. a. adverb, b. adjective, c. verb
2. a. adjective (or article), b. noun, c. preposition
3. a. noun, b. conjunction, c. noun
4. a. adjective, b. verb, c. pronoun
5. a. preposition, b. adjective, c. noun
6. a. adverb, b. verb, c. noun
7. a. verb, b. adverb, c. adverb
8. a. conjunction, b. adverb, c. preposition
9. a. verb, b. preposition, c. conjunction, d. adjective
10. a. adverb, b. adjective (or article), c. pronoun, d. adjective

Pages 42-43: Note-Taking and Summarizing: Chapters 7-8

Each chapter has at least one page for this activity. See *Summary of the Novel* (pgs. 111-113) for possible answers. *Student answers will always vary.*

Page 44: Comprehension Check: Chapters 7-8 *Answers will vary*

Chapter Seven

1. Newchildren are given a number which corresponds to the order in which they were born during the year. This number is preceded by the number of their current age group.
2. elected every ten years
3. The goal is to fit in, to standardize their behavior, to curb any impulse that might set them apart from the group
4. Excellent caretaker, tender with the Old, sensitive, gentle
5. One student is assigned to each job per year. This ensures that the community has a constant cycle of workers in each position.
6. Answers should include that specificity is important throughout the community, using precise language standardizes the language by eliminating slang, and precise language forces the speaker to examine and reveal his/her inner thoughts more clearly.
7. Asher was repeatedly struck with a discipline wand until it left marks on his legs. Answers will probably include that the punishment was too severe. The punishment traumatized Asher, and he stopped speaking for a time.
8. Assistant Director of Recreation; it seems like a perfect Assignment for Asher's personality and skills which affirms the Elders' wisdom in making Assignments.
9. Jonas's number is skipped.
10. Jonas thinks he may have forgotten his number; embarrassment; he wants to disappear; shame; assumes he has done something wrong; humiliated; afraid

Chapter Eight

1. Scattered applause, rather than a swell of excited applause
2. Uncertain about what may occur, and many of the community's rules and interactions contain an ominous tone or feeling; Answers may include anxious, frightened, uncertain, concerned.
3. Jonas planned to approach the stage with a jaunty, self-assured walk, but he ends up being clumsy and out-of-sorts.
4. with the Elders, but apart from them; older gentleman with a beard and pale eyes

5. Answers should include that a problem occurred with the last Receiver-in-Training which had negative consequences for the community.
6. The position can't be modified once it is assigned. The person is to be alone, apart during his training. It is the most honored job in the community.
7. Intelligence- top student; Integrity- follows the rules and willingly accepts chastisement; Courage- will undergo physical pain and will experience things that only the previous Receivers have experienced; Wisdom- ability to make important decisions; Capacity to See Beyond- sees something beyond what is experienced in the community
8. Jonas doesn't think he has the ability to See Beyond at first, but as he looks at the audience he experiences a flicker of something different.
9. Answers will vary, but should include reasons which support the students' answers.
10. thankful, proud, fearful

Pages 45-46: Standards Focus: Setting and Problem

1. A specific year is not given, but it occurs sometime in the future.
2. Seasons are not discussed. The Ceremony of Twelve takes place in December, so it is sometime in December or January.
3. The community uses the yearly December ceremonies to mark each year.
4. The weather is always the same.
5. There is no variation in the landforms that exist in the community.
6. All dwellings in the community are the same (except for The Giver's), and all the buildings serve a functional and communal purpose.
7. Just as the community's geography is all alike, the citizens are also expected to be exactly alike with minimal individualism.
8. There do not seem to be any religious or moral underpinnings for the community. There are rites of passage and ceremony, which may indicate to some that there is a religious aspect, but there is no recognizable religion evident.
9. The government controls all aspects of the citizens' lives. Citizens are not given a choice in life. They are assigned their jobs and families and are expected to live the life they are given without dissent. Even dreams, which can be the most individual and personal thoughts, are expected to be shared each morning.
10. The citizens are dependent on the government for all their needs. It is impossible for a government of the masses to be responsive to the needs and desires of individual citizens, and therefore individual needs, etc. are stifled by the government. This might create a problem when a person decides to do his or her own thing. The individual is cast away (released). A community that does not encourage or even accept personal desires rejects creativity, uniqueness, and individual thought. This results in a stagnant society without expression in the form of art, music, or literature, for example.
11. Citizens do not select a career, but it is assigned to them. All Assignments aid in fulfilling the overall needs of the community.
12. All citizens are monitored and observed. All dreams must be reported. There is also a curfew.
13. The citizens must consent to the government's rules and regulations. If a citizen does not want to live under these structures, there is minimal room for disagreement and dissension.

Pages 47-48: Assessment Preparation: Vocabulary in Context

Part b. Inference will vary. Parts of speech and definitions are given.

1. noun; high standing in other's opinions
2. adjective; relating or applying to things that have happened in the past
3. verb; turn away
4. adjective; mild; harmless
5. noun; laziness; lack of interest
6. adjective; all the people in a group agreeing with other
7. adverb; occurring naturally; without being planned

Pages 49-50: Standards Focus: Note-Taking and Summarizing: Chapters 9-10
Each chapter has at least one page for this activity. See *Summary of the Novel* (pgs. 111-113) for possible answers. *Student answers will always vary.*

Page 51: Comprehension Check: Chapters 9-10 *Answers will vary*
Chapter Nine
1. The training will be completely alone, and there is only one Receiver at a time.
2. They are uncertain how to treat Jonas, and the relationship becomes a bit awkward. People move aside and he thinks he hears whispers.
3. Lily plans to volunteer at the Nurturing Center since she already knows how to feed Gabriel.
4. Her name was designated Not-to-Be-Spoken, the highest degree of disgrace. She disappeared and no one in the community knows what happened to her.
5. Answers may include honors to which one is appointed and which only one person occupies at a time such as the Pope, a government cabinet position, Teacher of the Year, etc. Honors which one seeks, such as president, would not compare.
6. The Instructions are much shorter than for other Assignments, and they do not really explain what the Assignment entails. *Reactions will vary.*
7. At the end of each school day, Jonas is to go to his training and then go home. He no longer has any free time for recreation.
8. Answers may recommend pretending like Jonas never has dreams or doesn't remember them.
9. Answers may include unhappiness with your Assignment, not wanting to be in the community, etc.
10. It occurs to Jonas that other adults may be able to lie, and he may not always have been told the truth about things in the community.

Chapter Ten
1. The Attendant stands to acknowledge Jonas's presence.
2. The Receiver's dwelling has a lock, more luxurious furniture, and many more books. Other citizens' dwellings do not have locks, have only functional furniture, and have the same three books. The Receiver can also turn off the speaker in his dwelling, something the other citizens cannot do.
3. Jonas realizes that there could be rules beyond those that govern the community.
4. They both have pale (blue) eyes.
5. Jonas may ask questions of the Receiver, and neither of them may discuss the training with anyone else. The Receiver's job is to transmit to Jonas all the memories of the past.
6. He has memories of the whole world which go back many generations.
7. Jonas realizes that the world consists of more people than those in the community and began before the community.
8. The memories are like going downhill through deep snow on a sled; exhilarating at first, but as the snow/ memories build up, it gets more difficult to keep going.
9. He tells Jonas to remove his tunic and lie face down on the bed. The Receiver then places his hands on Jonas's back.

Pages 52-53: Standards Focus: Imagery
Answers will vary, but should include a description which adds more detail to the author's imagery.

Pages 54-55: Assessment Preparation: Verb Tense and Agreement *Answers for C will vary, but should be written in the tense indicated in C below.*
1. a. He, b. will imagine, c. past
2. a. It, b. was, c. present
3. a. she, b. seems, c. future
4. a. fabrics, b. are, c. future
5. a. I, b. failed, c. present
6. a. Jonas, b. will do, c. present
7. a. they, b. will study, c. past
8. a. name, b. indicates, c. future
9. a. He, b. wondered, c. present
10. a. He, b. will want, c. past

Pages 56-57: Standards Focus: Note-Taking and Summarizing: Chapters 11-12
Each chapter has at least one page for this activity. See *Summary of the Novel* (pgs. 111-113) for possible answers. *Student answers will always vary.*

Page 58: Comprehension Check: Chapters 11-12 *Answers will vary*

Chapter Eleven

1. Jonas sleds down a hill in the snow.
2. Jonas loves the feeling of sledding and enjoys his first experience with snow.
3. Answers should include things the student experienced for the first time such as riding a roller coaster, skateboarding, etc.
4. Jonas can see his surroundings with his eyes open, but he can also see and look around in the memories he receives.
5. The community is many generations old. Assuming that a generation is about twenty years, the community is probably at least one hundred years old.
6. snow, weather patterns, hills, sunshine
7. The Giver is honored because he has an important position, but he does not have the power to change anything.
8. When receiving a memory, Jonas can look around in and manipulate the items in the memory. The memory seems to be completely real to Jonas when he is receiving it, very similar to dreams that we experience.
9. He is now giving the memories, rather than receiving them.

Chapter Twelve

1. Gabriel sleeps very fitfully. He probably wakes up and fusses during the night.
2. Jonas dreams about sledding. In the dream, he feels like he is sledding toward a destination that he must somehow reach.
3. Jonas is not able to discuss his training with his classmates.
4. The Old are probably just punished for things which are typical of an elderly person. Punishing the old shows a lack of respect for elders and reinforces that the community does not respect people who no longer contribute to the work of the community.
5. The apple he was throwing with Asher, the faces in the audience, and Fiona's hair
6. Seeing beyond means that Jonas is aware of qualities which exist beyond the community. He can see colors which do not exist in the community, but do exist outside of it.
7. The Giver has memories which go back many generations and include things that he has not personally witnessed, similar to us learning about history. The other citizens only have memories of things that they have personally experienced.
8. Everything is the same and without color. There is no change in the terrain and colorless would probably indicate shades of white or gray.
9. Citizens in the community do not have to worry about food, shelter, crime, or jobs. All their basic needs are met. They gave up anything which creates individuality and beauty, including free choice, colors, art, and nature. Answers will vary about the trade-off, but most students will probably say that the trade-off was not worth it. Responses may differ, however. Students who come from an unstable background, refugees from a war-torn area for example, may prefer the stability of the community over the potentially destructive free choices of our world today.

Pages 59-60: Standards Focus: Elements of Style *Answers may vary*

1. A. factual tone-seem like she is just reporting facts, B. precise word choice, C. descriptive vocabulary; Effect: Helps the reader picture the scene more vividly as Jonas matter-of-factly opens his eyes after the transformation
2. A. descriptive vocabulary, B. sentence fragments; Effect: Make conversation more realistic; helps convey the urgency and awe with which Jonas tells his story
3. A. sentence fragments, repetition; Effect: strengthens the realism of Jonas's point of view since people think in fragments and emphasizes his feelings about his experience
4. A. sentence fragments, factual tone, B. unusual proper nouns; Effect: reinforces that the citizens accept everything in the community as facts not to be challenged; gives feeling of conversation; gives reader sense of importance of Titles of its citizens

Page 61: Assessment Preparation: Synonyms and Antonyms

Answers will vary. Suggested answers are given for the synonyms and antonyms.

1. synonym: flood; antonym: drip
2. synonym: mirth, joy; antonym: depression, sadness

3. synonym: old, old-fashioned; antonym: cutting-edge; brand new
4. synonym: flinching; antonym: holding; relaxing
5. synonym: warning; antonym: permission
6. synonym: confused, puzzled; antonym: expected
7. synonym: cleverly; antonym: humorlessly

Pages 62-63: Standards Focus: Note-Taking and Summarizing: Chapters 13-14
Each chapter has at least one page for this activity. See *Summary of the Novel* (pgs. 111-113) for possible answers. *Student answers will always vary.*

Page 64: Comprehension Check: Chapters 13-14 *Answers will vary*
Chapter Thirteen
1. Jonas sees them in flashes and the colors fade in and out.
2. Jonas wants to make choices and decisions for himself.
3. Answers will probably include examples of parents prohibiting their children from being in a situation where they could make a poor choice.
4. Answers should include details to support the students' opinions. Responses may include that a trade-off exists between the severity of the consequence and how appropriate it would be to be prevented from having a choice at all.
5. *Answers will vary*
6. Family units are created for the functional purpose of raising children, not because a couple loves each other. Spouses are paired, not self-selected because of an emotional bond. Couples then receive non-biological newchildren when the children are one year old. Once children leave home, the family unit no longer exists. The child disappearing in the river was the only mention of a death in the community and the Ceremony that followed served to minimize its importance. Citizens are discouraged from forming emotional attachments to each other.
7. The Receiver may not share or acknowledge any of the books, memories, or daily experiences with anyone, including his/her family unit.
8. Jonas says that a person's life is the things he/she does each day. The Elders view a person's life in regards to their function and usefulness in the community. The Giver believes that a person's life is his/her innermost being, his/her soul.
9. The community would probably cease to function as it does now. If the citizens were aware of other places, history, love, and families, they would probably question the community's ways and refuse to be controlled as they are now.

Chapter Fourteen
1. The previous sledding memories have been enjoyable, but this memory involves an injury and shows that sledding can also be dangerous. Since sledding is symbolic of freedom and escape, this memory shows that freedom and escape can also be dangerous.
2. The rules prohibit Jonas from taking medicine for any pain incurred while receiving memories. This forces Jonas to completely experience the memory.
3. The Citizens wanted to increase the birth rate to have more workers for the community, not to have more children to love and care for.
4. An increasing world population led to famine which escalated to a possible world war. To avoid this situation in the future, communities evolved which strictly limit population and control the citizens' lives to ensure that famine and war will not occur again.
5. The Giver and Receiver keep all the memories. This prevents citizens from knowing about any ways of life outside of the community. This lack of knowledge allows the Elders to maintain control of the community.
6. Answers should include realistic ideas which are feasible for Jonas and The Giver's situation.
7. Answers should include facts to support the students' arguments.
8. Gabriel can sit alone, reach for and grasp small play objects, has six teeth, is cheerful during the day, and seems to have normal intelligence. At night, however, he is fretful and needs frequent attention.

9. Jonas believes that Elsewhere is another community similar to his own. He thinks that everyone who has left his community lives in Elsewhere and will welcome and care for newcomers.
10. The first time Jonas does not intentionally transmit a memory of Gabriel. Jonas is startled and pulls away from Gabriel when he realizes that he transmitted a memory to the child. The second time Jonas intentionally transmits a memory of sailing to Gabriel to calm him.
11. Answers should include reasons to support the students' answers.

Pages 65-66: Standards Focus: Conflict
Explanations will vary

1. man vs. himself; Jonas struggles with the frustration that he is experiencing.
2. man vs. man; Lily resists when Jonas tries to transmit a memory to her.
3. man vs. society; The Giver struggles with the rules imposed on him by the community.
4. man vs. himself; Jonas challenges himself to see beyond.
5. man vs. nature; The forces of nature (snow, gravity, speed) overcome Jonas as he tries to control the sled.
6. man vs. man or man vs. society; War exemplifies men fighting against other men.
7. man vs. himself; Jonas tries to decide if he should tell The Giver about transmitting a memory to Gabriel. It bothers his conscience.

Page 67: Assessment Preparation: Vocabulary Extension
Sentences will vary

1. ominous
2. sinuous
3. agony
4. placidly
5. irrationally
6. embedded
7. assuage
8. assimilated

Pages 68-69: Standards Focus: Note-Taking and Summarizing: Chapters 15-17
Each chapter has at least one page for this activity. See *Summary of the Novel* (pgs. 111-113) for possible answers. *Student answers will vary.*

Page 70: Comprehension Check: Chapters 15-17 *Answers will vary*
Chapters Fifteen-Sixteen

1. Students learn about and know of history, while the Receiver personally experiences history as if he were a part of it.
2. Students should give reasons to support their answers.
3. Jonas is aware of history and life outside of the community. Because of his position, he has been somewhat separated from his classmates. The other students can still play like children since they are unaffected by the memories.
4. Positives: birthday parties, art, colors, making choices, animals, freedom, solitude, sledding, sun, love, family, holidays, gifts, grandparents; Negatives: death, grief, war, hunger, poaching, sunburn, getting hurt, risk
5. Extended families and connections across generations do not exist in the community. The elderly stay at the House of the Old. In our society, children frequently interact with their grandparents and great-grandparents. Several generations sometimes live together.
6. Answers will vary, but should include that Jonas is wrestling with wanting to experience the love and beauty of the outside world while still within the stability of the community. Jonas is trying to reconcile the positive and negative aspects of life outside the community.
7. Families depend on love to function properly and fulfill their purpose. Without love holding its members together, a family is just a way to raise children. It would be very difficult to go through all the chores and experiences of family life without love to make it worthwhile.
8. Jonas wishes The Giver could be his grandparent. It is possible that they are biologically related since they both have pale eyes, a rare trait in the community.
9. Everything involves some type of risk— risk of being rejected when we form a relationship with another person, risk of injury when driving or playing sports, risk of

not succeeding when we start a new job or try something new.

10. To be proud of someone means being pleased for a person when they succeed at something. Love is a deep feeling that exists whether the loved person succeeds or fails, behaves, or makes a mistake. Jonas's parents have pride in his accomplishments, but do not love him unconditionally as a parent should love a child. His parents do not understand love because they do not have the model of love that Jonas has seen in the memories.
11. Jonas admits that he wants the community to change so that the citizens can experience love and colors. Jonas conveys love to Gabriel by giving him pleasant memories.

Chapter Seventeen

1. Jonas can see colors all the time and is experiencing a new depth of feelings. He also sees the shallowness of the feelings experienced by others in the community.
2. The game brings back feelings of the memory of war that Jonas experienced.
3. Jonas realizes that he has become completely separated from his peers. He will no longer be able to interact and play with them as he once did.
4. Father must weigh the twins. He will then clean the smaller twin, perform a Ceremony of Release, and someone will take the child to Elsewhere.

Pages 71-73: Standards Focus: Theme

Answers may vary. Sample student answers are given. Suggested themes are given.

1. Jonas misses his childhood innocence, friendships, and feeling secure in the community.
2. Love creates the warmth of the scene. Without love, it is just another gathering of people, no different from the community. He sees people sharing and being close at a special time. He can really "feel" the love in the scene.
3. Jonas longs for the human connection he previously felt with his friends. In the memory, he realizes that love is the key to stronger human connections. It seems to be what he "sees" the most. He tries to establish this connection with Gabriel.

Theme: Human connection is a natural, necessary desire.

4. People in a group share something in common. Behavior and appearance are things that a person can control about himself to fit in with a group.
5. Birthday parties do not exist in the community. Children change age as a large group on the same day.
6. In the community, individuality is sacrificed to achieve conformity. Having individual jobs and personalities are the only types of individuality allowed.
7. In our world, people try to balance the two. Individuality is encouraged to a point, but people usually try to be individuals within their larger group.

Theme: Being an individual with unique thoughts and ideas is something we all desire.

8. The memories are affecting how he feels on a daily basis. He is becoming more mature and knowledgeable, and the memories are affecting how he sees his community and life.
9. The memories give Jonas a frame of reference that another way of life exists. They show him that there is an alternative to the community's way of living.
10. By not having memories, the community loses a feeling of connectedness between its citizens. They also lose the ability to refer to memories when making decisions. Lack of memories maintains the community's structure and rigidity. If the citizens had memories they would probably refuse to live within the rules and structures of the community.

Theme: Remembering the past is an important part of life and part of the growth of human beings.

11. Jonas sees that there is a danger in allowing people to have feelings and individual thought. He recognizes that with individual thought comes people who want to do their own thing. From that, he recognizes that people who have their own ideas will not work for the good of the community, but for their own gain.
12. Jonas wants the community to experience colors, true families, love, and memories.
13. *Answers will vary.* Be sure to discuss possible ways in which Jonas could change

his society. Discuss the positives and negatives of changing the community from within or leaving the community and trying to change it from the outside.

Theme: Sometimes, change and differences can be good things.

Pages 74-75: Assessment Preparation: Punctuation

1. "Put your hands on me," he directed, aware that in such anguish The Giver might need reminding.
2. In one ecstatic memory he had ridden a gleaming brown horse across a field that smelled of damp grass, and had dismounted beside a small stream from which both he and the horse drank cold, clear water.
3. "It seems to work pretty well that way, doesn't it? The way we do it in our community?" Jonas asked.
4. Thinking, as he always did, about precision of language, Jonas realized that it was a new depth of feelings that he was experiencing.
5. Now he had, in the memories, experienced injustice and cruelty and he had reacted with rage that welled up so passionately inside him that the thought of discussing it calmly at the evening meal was unthinkable.
6. "I'm the one who's training for Assistant Recreation Director," Asher pointed out angrily. "Games aren't your area of expertness."
7. Jonas trudged to the bench beside the Storehouse and sat down, overwhelmed with feelings of loss.
8. "Do you actually take it Elsewhere, Father?" Jonas asked.
9. "What is your favorite?" Jonas asked The Giver.
10. The small child went and sat on the lap of the old woman, and she rocked him and rubbed her cheek against his.

Pages 76-77: Standards Focus: Note-Taking and Summarizing: Chapters 18-20

Each chapter has at least one page for this activity. See *Summary of the Novel* (pgs. 111-113) for possible answers. *Student answers will always vary.*

Page 78: Comprehension Check: Chapters 18-20 *Answers will vary*

Chapter Eighteen

1. The Receiver may not request release.
2. They both were intelligent and eager to begin their Assignment. Instead of experiencing the painful memories, Rosemary requested release. Jonas has withstood the difficult memories.
3. Rosemary was stunned because the memory seemed inconceivable based on her experiences. In reality, all children in the community are taken from their parents.
4. Rosemary could not stand the physical and emotional pain associated with the memories.
5. The memories would be released into the community for everyone to experience.

Chapter Nineteen

1. The twins would be an anomaly and would not fit into the inflexible structures of the community. Ironically, identical twins would be exactly alike, a goal which the community embraces.
2. The Giver wants Jonas to understand exactly how the community functions, even if the truth is painful. *Reasoning will vary.*
3. Jonas's father injects the infant with a substance that kills the infant. Father commits infanticide.
4. Jonas had always been told that a release involves a beautiful ceremony before the person is released into the arms of someone from Elsewhere. The infant does not receive a ceremony. He is murdered, and his body is put into a box and disposed of. The Elderly do have a Ceremony of Release, however.
5. Jonas now looks at his father as a murderer and a liar.
6. Rosemary very likely understood that release really meant death. She chose to commit suicide rather than continue to experience the memories.

Chapter Twenty

1. Jonas is more attached to The Giver. Jonas wants The Giver to leave the community with him, but Jonas does not mention missing his family unit when he leaves.
2. The infant is sacrificed for the goals of the community, just as Jonas's peace of mind has been sacrificed for the goals of the community.

3. The memories gave Jonas the ability to feel true emotions and to imagine a better life for himself and the community. The memories also destroyed Jonas's sense of trust and security in the community.
4. The Giver plans to stay in the community to help the citizens process the memories.
5. The Giver experienced hearing beyond, hearing music.
6. Answers may include Jonas and The Giver seeing beyond and hearing beyond to see colors and hear music that currently occur outside of the community.
7. Jonas will leave his bicycle and clothes by the river so the community thinks that he drowned. Jonas will then hide in The Giver's vehicle when he visits another community and escape while he is in the other community.
8. Rosemary and The Giver both have pale eyes, a recessive genetic trait. The Giver believes that he will be with Rosemary when he is released.
9. The author foreshadows Jonas disappearing from the community. The Giver seems to be thinking of a plan for Jonas to release his memories into the community. The Giver wants to stay and help the community with the memories before he asks for release. Clues might include The Giver wants to be with Rosemary, Jonas refuses to go home, etc.

Pages 79-80: Standards Focus: Character Development

Sample answers are provided below. Students may utilize other passages to create the same effect.

1. "'I know there's really nothing to worry about,' Jonas explained, 'and that every adult has been through it. I know you have, Father, and you too, Mother. But it's the Ceremony that I'm apprehensive about. It's almost December.'" (pg. 9)
2. "'I don't know. I don't think anybody does, except the committee. He just bowed to all of us and then walked, like they all do, through the special door in the Releasing Room. But you should have seen his look. Pure happiness, I'd call it.'" (pg. 32)
3. "Like the Matching of Spouses and the Naming and Placement of newchildren, the Assignments were scrupulously thought through by the Committee of Elders.

   He was certain that his Assignment, whatever it was to be, and Asher's too, would be the right one for them." (pg. 49)
4. "But when he looked out across the crowd, the sea of faces, the thing happened again. The thing that had happened with the apple.

   They *changed*.

   He blinked, and it was gone. His shoulders straightened slightly. Briefly he felt a tiny sliver of sureness for the first time." (pg. 64)
5. "He leaned back, resting his head against the back of the upholstered chair. 'It's the memories of the whole world,' he said with a sigh. 'Before you, before me, before the previous Receiver, and generations before him.'

   Jonas frowned. 'The whole world?' he asked. 'I don't understand. Do you mean not just us? Not just the community? Do you mean Elsewhere, too?' He tried in his mind, to grasp the concept. 'I'm sorry, sir. I don't understand exactly. Maybe I'm not smart enough. I don't know what you mean when you say 'the whole world' or 'generations before him.' I thought there was only us. I thought there was only now.'

   'There's much more. There's all that goes beyond— all that is Elsewhere— and all that goes back, and back, and back.'" (pgs. 77-78)
6. "He was left, upon awakening, with the feeling that he wanted, even somehow needed, to reach the something that waited in the distance. The feeling that it was good. That it was welcoming. That it was significant." (pg. 88)
7. "'But why can't *everyone* have the memories? I think it would seem a little easier if the memories where shared. You and I wouldn't have to bear so much by ourselves, if everybody took a part.'

   The Giver sighed. 'You're right,' he said. 'But then everyone would be burdened and pained. They don't want that. And that's the real reason The Receiver is so vital to them, and so honored. They selected me— and you— to lift that burden from themselves.'

'When did they decide that?' Jonas asked angrily. "It wasn't fair. Let's change it!'" (pgs. 112-113)

8. "'It seems to work pretty well that way, doesn't it? The way we do it in our community?' Jonas asked. "I just didn't realize there was any other way, until I received that memory.'

   'It works,' The Giver agreed.

   Jonas hesitated. 'I certainly liked the memory, though. I can see why it's your favorite. I couldn't quite get the word for the whole feeling of it, the feeling that was so strong in the room.'

   'Love,' The Giver told him.

   Jonas repeated it. 'Love.' It was a word and concept new to him. (pg. 125)
9. "' I will take care of that, sir. I will take care of that, sir,' Jonas mimicked in a cruel, sarcastic voice. 'I will do whatever you like, sir. I will kill people, sir. Old people? Small newborn people? I'd be happy to kill them, sir. Thank you for your instructions, sir. How may I help y—' He couldn't seem to stop." (pg. 152-153)
10. *Answers will vary.* Be sure students use statements and quotes from the text to support their argument.

Pages 81-82: Assessment Preparation: Precise Word Choice
Answers will vary. Sample student answers are given.

1. a. The Giver hesitated painfully, as if saying the name aloud might hurt. "Her name was Rosemary," he told Jonas, finally.
   b. Excruciating involves a greater pain and conveys the depth of The Giver's feelings for Rosemary.
2. a. "I couldn't bring myself to cause her physical pain."
   b. Inflict tells the reader that The Giver is the actual person creating the pain, not just that he did something to make her experience it.
3. a. "I wish I could watch," he added later.
   b. An afterthought means that Jonas quickly added the comment to the conversation. Later could be any time in the future.
4. a. "I do know that I sat here numb with horror and feeling helpless."
   b. Wretched conveys that The Giver is overcome with feelings and greatly distressed. Feeling helpless just says that he knew he couldn't stop or help Rosemary.
5. a. "I am allowed to lie. But I have never lied to you."
   b. Allowed just means that The Giver can lie. Empowered invokes the power that The Giver has *because* he can lie.
6. a. "I think that they can, and that they will gain some wisdom."
   b. Acquire involves getting, taking hold of, and using the memories. Gaining just means they received wisdom.
7. a. Confronted by a situation which they had never faced before, and having no memories from which to find either relief or wisdom, they would not know what to do and would seek his advice.
   b. Solace involves receiving comfort which The Giver intends to provide to the community. Relief can imply making something go away.

Pages 83-84: Standards Focus: Note-Taking and Summarizing: Chapters 21-23
Each chapter has at least one page for this activity. See *Summary of the Novel* (pgs. 111-113) for possible answers. *Student answers will always vary.*

Page 85: Comprehension Check: Chapters 21-23 *Answers will vary*
Chapter Twenty-One

1. Jonas learns that Gabriel is going to be released the next morning.
2. Since Jonas stayed with The Giver, Father took Gabriel to the Nurturing Center for the night. Without Jonas to console and give him memories, Gabriel fussed and cried most of the night.
3. The author does not reveal that Gabriel is with Jonas until after she describes Jonas's flight from the community.
4. Answers may include that citizens may not leave their dwellings so that all their movements are controlled and accounted for. There may be a finite amount of food so it must be rationed.
5. *Discuss the feasibility of some of the students' plans.*
6. Jonas truly loves, cares for, and tries to meet Gabriel's needs as an individual. The Nurturers did not truly nurture Gabriel.

They tried to make him fit into their standards and chose to release Gabriel when he would not conform to what they expected.

7. When the novel opens, Jonas is frightened and seeks shelter when an unauthorized plane flies over the community. At the novel's close, Jonas is again frightened and seeks shelter when planes fly overhead. This time the planes are looking for him, however. Purposes will vary, but might include that the first instance of the plane foreshadowed the ending of the novel.
8. The plan seems to work since Jonas's memories fade as he gets farther away from the community.
9. Jonas can alter his body temperature based on the memory that he is thinking about.
10. *Answers will vary.* They have possibly traveled 100-200 miles and are probably in outlying lands from the community. It is disconcerting that they have traveled so far and not come to any other towns.

Chapter Twenty-Two

1. The landscape becomes more varied with forests, hills, and waterfalls. They experience rain and see animals.
2. Jonas realizes that Gabriel's survival depends on Jonas keeping him safe and healthy. Jonas sacrifices himself for Gabriel. Father sacrifices Gabriel because he will not fit into the community's artificial behavioral standards.
3. While fleeing, Jonas scrounges for food and catches fish to eat. In the community, food was delivered each day without any effort from the citizens. His survival due to natural forces is truly in doubt outside of the community. In the community, he would die from release, not from natural forces.
4. Jonas cares about saving Gabriel more than he cares about saving himself.

Chapter Twenty-Three

1. *Answers will vary.* Discuss the clues which could lead to each possibility.
2. Gabriel is now lethargic and dirty. In the community, he was curious, alert, and happy.
3. *Answers will vary.*
4. *Answers will vary.* Discuss the clues which could lead to each possibility.
5. Answers will vary, but Jonas always felt that Elsewhere truly existed. We know that it is December, and Jonas thinks he sees Christmas lights in the town. Discuss the symbolism of Gabriel's name, as well the author's comment that "they were waiting, too, for the baby."
6. Other possibilities could include that Jonas is dying and going to heaven, he is going into his favorite memory, hallucinating, or really escaping and going to a town at Christmas-time.

Page 86: Standards Focus: Elements of Plot

Exposition: the community; Jonas's friends and family unit prepare for the upcoming Ceremony; Jonas is assigned to be the Receiver. Gabriel begins staying with Jonas's family unit overnight.

Rising Action: Jonas trains as the Receiver. Through the memories, Jonas learns about history and life before and outside of the community. The more memories Jonas gains, the more dissatisfied he becomes with the community. Jonas transfers memories to Gabriel to soothe him at night.

Climax: Jonas witnesses his Father releasing a newborn, and realizes that release means death. Father tells the family unit that Gabriel is going to be released.

Falling Action: Jonas takes Gabriel and escapes from the community.

Resolution: The resolution is ambiguous. Jonas and Gabriel are sledding downhill toward a town, but the reader is unsure if they have escaped from the community or died.

Page 87: Assessment Preparation: Sentence Structure

1. simple sentence; subject- he; verb- could see
2. simple sentence with a compound verb; subject- Jonas; verb- put, stared
3. compound sentence; subject- they; verb- were; subject- he; verb- stopped
4. simple sentence with a compound subject; subject- Instructor, class; verb- waited
5. simple sentence with a compound verb; subject- Jonas; verb- knelt, tried
6. simple sentence; subject-memory; verb- was
7. compound sentence; subject- they; verb- had; subject- they; verb- had

Page 88: Quiz: Chapters 1-2

1. b. go inside
2. a. apologize to the entire class
3. d. He does not sleep soundly at night.
4. b. reward
5. c. tell their feelings
6. a. ceremony when each child gets older
7. d. at the Nurturing Center
8. b. calls him by the name he will be given
9. a. children stop going to school
10. c. Receiver

Page 89: Quiz: Chapters 3-4

1. Since Birthmothers have 3 births in 3 years and then do manual labor for the remainder of their lives, they are viewed as unintelligent.
2. Citizens want to be as similar to others as possible without showing any individuality.
3. He notices something different about the apple and wants to examine it more closely.
4. Students individual talents and qualities are pointed out at the Ceremony of Twelve. A person's accomplishments are lauded at a Ceremony of Release.
5. An Assignment is the job which a citizen will perform until he goes to live in the House of the Old.
6. food, clothing, home, job, education, bicycle for transportation, childcare

Page 90: Vocabulary Quiz: Chapters 1-4

1. c. the opposite of intended or expected meaning
2. f. noticeable; intense; obvious
3. a. to influence someone through flattery or trickery
4. h. personality; attitude
5. g. breaking a law or rule
6. d. brought up feelings of amazement or fear
7. b. strictly; based on a legal interpretation
8. e. natural ability
9. n. to correct or punish
10. k. in a touchy, sullen, or grumpy manner
11. p. a strong feeling of guilt
12. i. belief
13. o. move or act quickly
14. l. calculated
15. j. annoying or unpleasant
16. m. laughed; giggled

Page 91: Quiz: Chapters 5-6

1. false; At breakfast each morning, the family unit tells their dreams; OR, At dinner they tell their feelings.
2. true
3. true
4. false; The December Ceremony is the major celebration in the community.
5. false; Caleb fell in the river and drowned.
6. true
7. false; At the age of one, newchildren are placed with a family and *assigned* a name. Families do not select their own children's names.
8. false; Twelves are given an Assignment.
9. true

Page 92: Quiz: Chapters 7-8

1. b. identified by a number corresponding to the order in which they were born
2. a. elected every ten years
3. c. Assistant Director of Recreation
4. d. the Elders meticulously observe the students
5. b. the person may refuse the Assignment
6. a. Intelligence, Integrity, Courage, Wisdom, and the Capacity to See Beyond

Page 93: Vocabulary Quiz: Chapters 5-8

1. reprieve
2. avert
3. meticulously
4. prestige
5. disquieting
6. spontaneously
7. exuberant
8. indolence
9. emblem
10. profound
11. infringed
12. benign
13. unanimous
14. relinquish
15. retroactive

Page 94: Quiz: Chapters 9-10

1. Go immediately to the Annex at the end of the school day. Go immediately to your dwelling after training. You are exempted from rules governing rudeness. Do not discuss your training with anyone else. You are prohibited from dream-telling. Do not

apply for medication for training-related injuries. You may not apply for release. You may lie.
2. Her name was designated Not-to-Be-Spoken, the highest form of disgrace. She disappeared from the community, and no one knows what happened to her.
3. He will go to his training at the end of the school day and then go immediately home. He no longer has any free time to spend with his friends.
4. It has a lock, luxurious furniture, and many books. The speaker can also be turned off.
5. He realizes that there may be life outside of and previous to the community.
6. Jonas may ask the Receiver questions. The Receiver is to transmit all memories of the world to Jonas by placing his hands on Jonas's bare back.

Page 95: Quiz: Chapters 11-12

1. false; Sledding down a hill is the first memory Jonas receives.
2. false; Jonas cannot change the things that occur in his memories.
3. true
4. false; Jonas is to now call his mentor The Giver.
5. true
6. false; Seeing Beyond means that Jonas can see colors and aspects of items that other citizens cannot see.
7. true
8. false; The community's citizens cannot see colors, only shades of gray and white.

Page 96: Vocabulary Quiz: Chapters 9-12

1. b. large group of people
2. e. getting off something, such as a horse or bicycle
3. h. appreciation; enjoyment
4. d. necessary; essential
5. a. source; beginning
6. g. small recessed section of a room
7. f. one that follows another in a job or office
8. c. with fear or trepidation; suspiciously
9. m. flood; rapid outpouring
10. k. high-spirited joy
11. o. no longer useful
12. i. flinching away from pain
13. l. buying and selling of goods
14. p. strong advice; warning
15. j. puzzled; confused
16. n. cleverly; with humor and irony

Page 97: Quiz: Chapters 13-14

1. c. He sees flashes of red.
2. a. He tries to give a memory of an elephant to Lily.
3. d. The elephant is poached and mourned by another elephant.
4. b. He has to travel a lot.
5. c. Jonas falls off the sled and gets hurt.
6. d. He sleeps through the night.
7. b. Jonas gives Gabriel a soothing memory to help him sleep.

Page 98: Quiz: Chapters 15-17

1. In our society, several generations of family members interact with each other. In the community, there is no such thing as grandparents or extended families. The elderly live at the House of the Old and do not maintain contact with their family unit.
2. The Giver's favorite memory is of several generations of a family gathered at Christmas. There is a tree with twinkling lights and a feeling of love in the room.
3. Jonas tells Gabriel that he wants the community to change so that everyone can experience love and colors.
4. He can see colors all the time and experiences deeper feelings.
5. Jonas gets upset and tries to get his friends to stop playing the game.
6. Father will weigh the twins. He will then clean the smaller twin, perform a Ceremony of Release, and someone will take the smaller twin to Elsewhere.

Page 99: Vocabulary Quiz: Chapters 13-17

1. ominous
2. permeated
3. sinuous
4. anguish
5. embedded
6. expertise
7. placidly
8. wisp
9. irrationally
10. glum
11. agony
12. injustice
13. assuage

14. ecstatic
15. assimilated
16. trudged

Page 100: Quiz: Chapters 18-20

Answers may vary

1. true; *some will say false. He is allowed to request release once the new Receiver is trained.*
2. true
3. false; If Jonas disappeared, the memories would be released into the community.
4. false; The Giver encourages Jonas to watch the video of the infant's release.
5. true
6. false; The Giver plans to stay in the community to help the citizens process the memories. Jonas plans to leave alone.
7. true
8. false; Jonas plans to put his clothes by the river so that it looks like he drowned. He plans to escape from the community in The Giver's vehicle.

Page 101: Quiz: Chapters 21-23

1. a. spends the night at The Giver's dwelling.
2. c. Jonas must take Gabriel with him when he flees.
3. d. He rides his father's bicycle.
4. b. Jonas and Gabriel see more animals and varied weather.
5. a. a sled
6. c. twinkling lights and singing

Page 102: Vocabulary Quiz: Chapters 18-23

1. c. very unhappy; dispirited; disappointed
2. h. extremely painful
3. e. to cause or impose; to deal or mete out
4. a. an idea occurring later
5. d. in a state of great hardship; miserable
6. g. gave authority or power to
7. b. to get or obtain possession
8. f. relief from emotional distress or grief
9. k. splashing or turning violently
10. n. feeling, showing, or causing regret or pity
11. i. without energy; slow and sluggish
12. l. made greater or more numerous
13. p. watchful and alert
14. o. teasing by showing something desirable but continually out of reach
15. j. slowed the progress of; interfered
16. m. very heavy; like lead

Pages 103-106: Final Test

1. e. assigned to be the Receiver-in-Training
2. h. works as a Nurturer
3. j. works at the Department of Justice
4. a. Jonas's younger sister
5. c. assigned to be Assistant Director of Recreation
6. i. assigned as a Caretaker of the Old
7. b. newchild who does not sleep well at night
8. f. holds the community's memories
9. d. previous Receiver-in-Training
10. g. lives at the House of the Old
11. false
12. true
13. true
14. false
15. true
16. false
17. true
18. true
19. false
20. false
21. true
22. false
23. a. reward
24. d. has three children and then performs manual labor
25. b. a car
26. d. the Elders
27. c. sense of humor
28. a. You may not lie.
29. c. different types of food
30. d. sleeping through the night
31. b. a family at Christmas
32. c. heard music
33. b. Jonas misses his family unit
34. Answers should include specific examples such as spouses are selected, children are given, jobs are assigned, and all the citizens must abide by strict rules governing their freedom.
35. At the beginning of the novel, Jonas has complete faith in the community and its Elders, evidenced by the confidence he has in the Elders making Assignments. As he learns more about the outside world, Jonas resents the community and its structures more and more. By the end of the novel, Jonas rebels against the community and tries to escape. By leaving the community, Jonas releases his memories which will

probably lead other citizens to question the community and its structure.

36. Jonas cares about his family unit, but is crushed when his parents do not say they love him. Jonas and The Giver create a true relationship built on mutual caring, not an artificially-created family unit. Ironically, Jonas and The Giver are probably biologically related due to their pale eyes. After seeing his father commit infanticide, Jonas no longer wants to see his family unit, but begs The Giver to leave the community with him.
37. f. the opposite of intended or expected meaning
38. i. natural ability
39. a. to correct or punish
40. j. delay of punishment
41. m. very carefully; precisely
42. b. relating or applying to things that have happened in the past
43. n. mild; harmless
44. c. source; beginning
45. l. high-spirited joy
46. d. no longer useful
47. h. absorbed; understood
48. k. unfair treatment
49. e. relief from grief or anxiety
50. g. made greater or more numerous

Pages 107-110: Final Test: Multiple Choice

1. c. assigned to be Receiver-in-Training
2. a. works as a Nurturer
3. b. works in the Department of Justice
4. c. Jonas's younger sister
5. c. Assistant Director of Recreation
6. d. Assigned as a Caretaker of the Old
7. a. does not sleep well at night
8. d. holds the community's memories
9. b. previous Receiver-in-Training
10. c. lives at the House of the Old
11. c. tell their feelings
12. a. reward
13. b. All children become a year older.
14. c. gives birth three times, then performs hard labor the rest of her life
15. b. a car
16. d. performing volunteer hours
17. d. are identified by a number
18. d. the Elders
19. d. the Elders meticulously observe the students.
20. c. Sense of Humor
21. a. You may not lie.
22. b. Her name was designated Not-to-Be-Spoken.
23. c. The Giver
24. c. sledding downhill
25. c. different types of food
26. b. red
27. b. Jonas gives Gabriel a soothing memory to help him sleep.
28. d. sleeping through the night
29. b. a family at Christmas
30. c. heard music
31. a. in the back of The Giver's vehicle
32. b. Jonas misses his family unit.
33. b. Jonas and Gabriel see animals and varied weather.
34. a. ironic
35. d. chastise
36. c. retroactive
37. a. origin
38. c. obsolete
39. b. injustice
40. d. solace
41. c. aptitude
42. a. reprieve
43. b. benign
44. d. glee
45. b. assimilated
46. c. throng
47. b. scrupulously
48. d. indolence
49. a. augmented
50. d. successor